PLAIN JANE

For Sally

Best Wishes

Plain Jane

PLAIN JANE

Her Memoirs

(With apologies to A.P. Herbert)

Jane Donaldson

Book Guild Publishing
Sussex, England

First published in Great Britain in 2012 by
The Book Guild Ltd
Pavilion View
19 New Road
Brighton, BN1 1UF

Typesetting in Garamond by
Ellipsis Digital Ltd, Glasgow

Printed and bound in Great Britain by
CPI Group (UK) Ltd, Croydon, CR0 4YY

A catalogue record for this book is available from
The British Library.

ISBN 978 1 84624 756 9

PLAIN JANE

By A.P. Herbert

Jane! Jane!
Beautiful Jane!
Others may call you plain
But beauty is hidden in curious shapes;
People have found some attraction in apes;
Some love the lily and some like the leaf,
Some adore mutton and some prefer beef;
Brighton is beautiful, seen from the sea,
And you from all angles are lovely to me,
My Jane! Jane!
Beautiful, beautiful, beautiful, beautiful Jane!

This book is dedicated to all my forbears,
who made me what I am
— and to my two brave aviators

Chapter One

My great-grandmother, Emily Edith Grant, was born in Dum Dum near Calcutta on the 27th June 1857, on the very day that the Indian Mutiny broke out in that city – the city renowned for the Dum-dum bullet, which was one of the contentious factors that led the native troops to revolt, refusing to use bullets that they claimed were 'greased with the fat of sacred cows'. To escape assassination, the newborn baby and her mother were hidden by their loyal Indian servants under sacks in a bullock cart and smuggled to safety in Agra, home of the infant's grandparents. Her mother's Bible was lost on the journey and was later found by an Englishman, who sent it to her father with condolences – thinking that its owner had been murdered!

One of my great-great-grandmothers was the sister of tunnelling Kavanagh VC, who risked his life to relieve the besieged garrison of Lucknow, so I have very personal links with this dreadful time of hatred, savagery and revenge and a passionate interest in the events and personalities involved in that bloodthirsty period in the history of British India.

The Ridge is a rocky scrub-covered hill a couple of miles to the north of Old Delhi. It was the scene of one of the longest, bloodiest and most strategic battles of the Mutiny that, once won, enabled our troops to re-capture Delhi's Red Fort and relieve the garrison under siege there. The fighting, under foul conditions of

1

heat, flies, disease and the stench of gunpowder and decaying flesh, lasted for more than four days. Some of the most violent episodes took place on the crest of The Ridge, in and around a mansion belonging to an Indian merchant loyal to the Raj, one Hindu Rau (see map). Hindu Rau was a man of considerable substance and stature in Delhi. His house was an elegant one, set in beautifully laid-out gardens. After the Mutiny had been quelled, the gardens were restored to their former glory, and after Hindu Rau died, the house was converted into a British nursing home. It was in this by then tranquil setting, on the 27th February 1932, that I came into the world – on exactly the same day and at almost the same moment as Miss Elizabeth Taylor was being delivered in London.

My father, a captain in the Royal Artillery, was at that time stationed in Ambala in the Punjab, but he came down to Delhi for the confinement, staying at the Swiss Hotel in Old Delhi. I think the Devil must already have been within me at birth, for I arrived with hairy points on the tips of my ears and a 'tail' at the base of my spine! Fortunately, these unusual accessories vanished almost at once. After two peaceful weeks in the Hindu Rau hospital – Delhi's climate in February and March is very pleasant – my father drove us all the way back to our bungalow at 73 Northbrook Road, Ambala.

These were the twilight days of the Raj, and although its death-throes were approaching, my infancy and early childhood were spent among the comforts and privileges that were still there to be enjoyed and taken for granted. My memories of India in those days are few, but they are deeply engraved. We lived in spacious Victorian bungalows with shady verandahs, set in tidy and well-watered gardens. In the evenings, in the coolness of dusk, *chota pegs* (short drinks) and *burra pegs* (long drinks) would be served on the verandah to my parents and their friends, relaxing after tennis, polo, swimming or bridge. I had *ayahs* (nursemaids) to look after me – and I spoke, at one time, Hindustani as well as I spoke English. We had a *khansama* (cook), a *kitmugar* (butler) and a sweeper

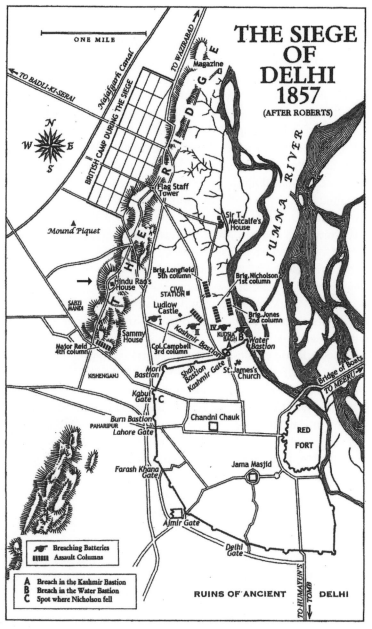

ONE MILE

TO BADLI-KI-SERAI

TO WAZIRABAD

Najafgarh Canal

BRITISH CAMP DURING THE SIEGE

N
W E
S

THE SIEGE
OF
DELHI
1857
(AFTER ROBERTS)

Magazine

R I D G E

JUMNA RIVER

Flag Staff
Tower

Sir T.
Metcalfe's
House

Mound Piquet

Brig. Longfield
5th column

Brig. Nicholson
1st column

T H E   R I D G E

Hindu Rao's
House

CIVIL
STATION

SABZI
MANDI

Ludlow
Castle

I

Sammy
House

Major Reid
4th column

KISHENGANJ

Kashmir Bastion

II

IV

KUDSIA
BAGH

Brig. Jones
2nd column

B   Water
Bastion

A

Col. Campbell
3rd column

Mori
Bastion

Shah
Bastion
Kashmir Gate

St. James's
Church

Bridge of Boats

TO MEERUT

Kabul
Gate   C

Burn Bastion
PAHARIPUR
Lahore Gate

Chandni Chauk

RED

FORT

Farash Khana
Gate

Jama Masjid

Ajmir Gate

Delhi
Gate

Breaching Batteries
Assault Columns

A   Breach in the Kashmir Bastion
B   Breach in the Water Bastion
C   Spot where Nicholson fell

RUINS OF ANCIENT

DELHI

TO HUMAYUN'S
TOMB

(from the lowest of castes – he emptied the bathtubs and thunderboxes and did all the most menial tasks). Our gardens were tended by *malis*, and when I was only four I had a *syce* to care for my pony, 'Funny Face', and to guide me with a leading rein. Funny Face was aptly named; he was the most loveable but dwarf-like and ugly-bodied pony!

In May of 1932, when I was three months old, we travelled to Mussoorie, a hill-station in the foothills of the Himalayas, to get away from the heat of the plains. The Savoy Hotel in Mussoorie had once been the 'summer residence' of my great-grandfather, Charles Coleman Dillon, a High Court judge in the city of Allahabad, father of Edith and George Wentworth. Great Grandfather Dillon had the same suite of rooms reserved for him every summer, and his own private shady spot in the garden beneath two Deodar trees, where he would sit for most of the day holding court and enjoying the panorama of the Doon Valley spread out 5000 feet below.

I returned to Mussoorie fifty-two years later, in 1984, with my mother, my sister and my brother-in-law, Robin Glover, to find the Savoy virtually unchanged. It is a perfectly preserved Victorian hotel, and the two Deodar trees still shade the lawn overlooking the river.

Great Grandfather Dillon's winter habitat was 33 Canning Road in Allahabad, where among his friends and colleagues he numbered Motilal Nehru, father of Jamahlilal Nehru. He had been born in Subathu in the Simla Hills on the 6th August 1848. He died in 1938 at the Leinster Court Hotel in Bayswater, where he had spent his last few years almost blind and very lonely, cared for by his old Indian servant who had refused to be parted from him when he left the subcontinent. Tragedy had hit the old man late in his life when in 1927, his son, George, was killed by a tiger. The traumatic event was described in a letter to the authorities:

6 Hastings Road, Allahabad
25th March '27

Respected Sir,

I beg to submit that my master G.W. Dillon went tiger
shooting in Chawir jungle near Markundi Station on the
16th of March and having come back breath his last on the
24th of March about which I gave you a telegram
yesterday. The whole facts of the tragedy stand thus:

On the 22nd of March, the tiger committed murry[1] and
having taking to a distance of about half a furlong, left it
there. As soon as he got this news, he arranged for Hanka
on the morning of 23rd. The Hanka brought him round
before Mr Dillon. Mr Dillon shot and apparently killed his
animal; but the tiger fled away. Afterwards having come
down from the hill from where he shot; ordered Hanka
wala to climb the tree and himself went out in search of
the tiger about noon. He went about a furlong tracing the
blood of the tiger. There the tiger saw him and ran towards
him. Mr Dillon saw him coming towards him again, who
attacked him on the left thigh with one of his paws and
having caught hold of the gun, which was in his hand, with
another paw smashed its kunda with his teeth. In the
course of smashing, the bullet having come out of the
barrel hit his same thigh. The tiger after doing this went
back to about ten yards. The tiger died after half an hour
grumbling. Jahangir bearer and some shikaris having heard
the shot went to the Sahib who was at that time calling
'jahangir'. He was taken to tent four miles from the place
on a charpoi and from there he was taken on a bed to
Markundi station. There he wired the Chief Justice who
arranged for a special train on the night of 23rd. He caught

[1] Killed a man.

train from Markundi to Manikpore station, came down
from it for medical help, which was obtained. The doctor
did not take much interest seeing that the case was hopeless, owing to loss of blood through the thigh. About
3 a.m. on 24th he got the special train from Manikpore and
alighted at Allahabad Junction at 4 a.m. He was removed to
civil hospital and there he breath his last at 10 a.m. leaving
no unsupported. The same evening recremation took place.
His body was burnt according to his will and most probably his and tiger's tomb will be erected there, where the
tragedy took place.

While deploring his untimely death our sympathy goes to
his widow and his aged father who in his eightieth year has
to mourn the death of his only son.

Yours most obediently,

Mukat Behari Lal
Clerk of the Late Mr G.W. Dillon, Bar. At Law, Allahabad

Originally my maternal ancestors – Dillons, Keelans and Grants –
had come from Southern Ireland, from Swords near Dublin, from
Cloonah and from Ennis, County Clare. In the eighteenth century,
lack of opportunities at home caused them to travel to India to
forge their careers, and there, for several generations, the family
prospered. One elderly Keelan uncle, Jim, was still living in
Mussoorie when we returned to the Savoy Hotel in 1984. All his
roots were in India and he had 'stayed on'.

Luke Keelan was the eldest son of one of the first of the clan
to make his career in India. Born in Fort William (Calcutta), he
worked as a surveyor on the great Survey of India being carried
out in the late eighteenth and early nineteenth centuries. His eldest
son, Henry, was born there in 1817 and he, too, became a surveyor.
As a junior assistant he was assigned to help Colonel Everest in
his work on the massive task of surveying the subcontinent. He
was evidently an unsatisfactory assistant on many occasions and

incurred the wrath of the colonel for such ineptitudes as failing to shine his 'lights' at the appointed times. In spite of these early shortcomings, Henry did well and eventually rose to be Deputy Surveyor General of India – his name can be seen on many of the original maps of the country preserved in the British Museum. The following extract is from the book *Historical Records of the Survey of India* by R.H. Phillimore:

> Henry Keelan was a first-class officer in every way, and had been one of Everest's most trusted young assistants on the Great Arc (IV, 384). He particularly distinguished himself running a minor series of triangles through the tremendous Himalayan gorges of the Sutej and Spiti rivers during 1851–2, and did good work in charge of detachment on the Great Indus series, 1858–60 (48–9, 203–4). He spent season 1860–3 on the Ranum series in Rajputana, being promoted to First Assistant on Rs 618 in May 1861. He continued to hold charge of important parties till his retirement at the age of fifty-seven after special extensions of service. His son Henry Elliott carried on the good name for another twenty years.

But the following correspondence, extracted from the same publication, indicates that in his early work he was less laudable. From a letter sent by Colonel Everest to Keelan, 11th March 1833:

> I have seen two of your blue lights, but only got an angle with one because your time was so irregular ... I lost all your others, for the obvious reason that I was looking out for Mr Dove's lights at Dholri ... You are the cause of the detention of the camp by this neglect of my orders. The other day when I ordered you to commence at four, you did not commence till past five, and now when I ordered you to commence at five, you begin half an hour before ...
>   If you had seen how punctually and regularly both Mr Dove at Dholri and Shekh Ahmed at Saroli burned their lights, you

would sink into the ground for shame, and, truly, it is most disgraceful that the Naik of my guard can do cleverly what one of the Sub-Assistants of the G.T. (Great Trigonometric) Survey is quite unequal to ...

I send for your perusal a copy of a letter which I have written to Mr Dove. When shall I be able to write such a letter to you? Yet Mr Dove has not been six months in the G.T. Survey, and has no advantage over you, except that he is alert, and desirous to do his duty.

Everest scoffed at poor Keelan's admission that he had no watch:

No decent person is ever without a watch, and a man who has no watch can never pretend to be respectable. You ought to be ashamed to acknowledge that you have no watch. You might just as well say that you have no coat or no shoes or no hat. It is an essential part of the apparel, even of a stage coach driver.

Writing to Keelan again on the 22nd March:

You are evidently one of those uncertain people in whom no sort of confidence ever can be placed. Admonition and remonstrance are quite lost upon you, and it is plain that if you do not change your conduct, you never will be of the smallest use in this department.

Ask yourself, of what use a person can be who commits blunders so often that when any business is entrusted to him he fails twice out of three times. This is precisely your case. Sometimes you are too lazy to get up in the morning. At other times you make intervals of thirty-two minutes instead of sixteen. At other times you break the pole. In short, you never succeed except by the merest chance.

All this is very disgraceful to you, and I should certainly recommend you to look out for some other employment, for in the G.T. Survey you will never be of any use, and you only occupy the place of some more valuable person.

Later he redeemed himself, and Everest was to write:

Mr Keelan has not only shewn much contrition, but has conducted himself so much to my satisfaction, and attended so steadily to his duty . . .

Henry Keelan married Catherine Mary Anne Kavanagh, the afore-mentioned sister of Kavanagh VC, hero of the Siege of Lucknow in 1857. In the fashion of that time, Henry begat thirteen children, one of whom, Eugène, was born back home in Ireland at Swords, County Dublin, on the 7th March 1846, but he too made his career in India, as did *his* son Herman – who also 'stayed on' in Mussoorie after Independence. Another of Eugène's sons was my grandfather Douglas Keelan – or 'Buddha' as he was always known to me. He was born in Unas in the United Provinces (now Uttar Pradesh) of northern India on the 27th February 1879 (we shared the same birthday). Douglas married Edith Dillon ('Buddhi' to me), daughter of Charles Coleman Dillon, the High Court judge, and Emily, the infant of Dum Dum. They produced two daughters – Barbara, my mother (born on the 12th May 1910 at her grandparents' home at Canning Road, Allahabad), and Pamela, born in Lucknow eleven years later.

Douglas carved himself a successful career on the East Indian Railway and rose to elevated rank within the company. He was provided with his own railway coach fitted out with a well-furnished bedroom, day saloon, bathroom and kitchen, with separate living quarters for the servants who accompanied him. When he wished to travel any distance, either for work or for pleasure, the coach would be attached to a scheduled train and he would be conveyed to his destination in considerable comfort.

Social life in Mussoorie was hectic in 1932. Tennis parties; tea dances; riding; trekking in the wooded valleys; rickshaw rides; dancing every Saturday night in the ballrooms of the Savoy or Charleville hotels. My parents always stayed at the latter establishment, as at that time the Savoy had earned itself rather a 'fast' reputation. Unmarried residents had to be lodged in either the bachelors' or spinsters' wings in an attempt to preserve the proprieties, and the story goes that at 6 a.m. each morning a bell would be rung as a signal for corridor-creepers to return to their own rooms.

When I was a year old, we sailed from Bombay on board the *Viceroy of India* for a year's home leave, arriving at Tilbury on the 8th May. We stayed at the Leinster Court Hotel in Bayswater, where I met my Great Grandfather Dillon, then eighty-five and blind. From London we travelled by train from Euston to Glasgow and on to The Grange, Bridge-of-Weir, home of my paternal grand-parents, William and Winifred ('Winnie') Auld. During the year's leave, trips were also made to Bexhill-on-Sea and to Jersey, where my mother's parents had now retired to live at the Woodville Hotel in St Helier.

At the beginning of July 1934 we embarked from Birkenhead for the return journey to India, back on board the *Viceroy of India*, spending the night before departure at the Exchange Hotel in Liverpool. Once we reached Bombay we transferred to the SS *Barala* to sail for Karachi. My father was to spend three months back on the North West Frontier, and during his posting there we lodged at the Alexandra Hotel in Quetta – another social centre of Anglo-Indian life. Not long afterwards it was devastated by the violent earthquake of 1936.

Families were always on the move in India, following fathers and husbands to their various postings. Our next move was to 4 Ghangora in Dehra Dun, a military town (and also home of The Doon School, one of India's most famous public schools) in the valley below Mussoorie, where we stayed until November before packing our bags for a visit to a tented military camp at Kheri.

Our accommodation at Kheri was surprisingly comfortable and civilised, even if it was under canvas. My father at the time had a dearly loved Airedale dog called Sally, who had been with him since his bachelor days. Sally was devoted to the family and particularly protective towards me, the baby. One afternoon, when I had been put to rest in my cot, a rampaging pi-dog strayed into the tent. Sally immediately leapt to my defence and tried to see off the mangy visitor. A terrible dog fight took place around my cot until help arrived and the animals were wrenched apart. Sally had been quite severely bitten, the pi-dog had foam round its mouth, and some of its blood and saliva had splashed on to everything in the tent, including me, screaming in my cot. Naturally, the possibility that the pi-dog might have been rabid could not be ignored, and the danger that Sally could have been infected was a real one.

My poor father had only one option. Loading his revolver he took both dogs out into the jungle to do what had to be done. The dogs' bodies were sent off immediately to the Rabies Research Institute in Kasauli for post-mortem examination, but after tests, which took several days to conclude, neither was found to be infected with the dreaded disease. In the meantime, however, all of us who had had contact with the dog or its blood and saliva had to attend the clinic daily for the next two weeks to undergo a course of anti-rabies treatment. This was most unpleasant and painful, involving massive injections of vaccine into the abdomen, which soon became swollen and very uncomfortable. Being the youngest, I was privileged to be the first to be injected each day – with a fresh needle while it was still sharp.

Christmas that year we spent in Madras, where my father found and purchased what was to become a much-travelled car – a Vauxhall known as The Grumble-Box. From Madras, after Christmas, we drove in the Vauxhall to Bangalore in South India, where we were to stay until October 1935, first at 1a Residency Road and later at 19 Cambridge Road. It was here that I was given my first pony, Funny Face, and was entered in the Bangalore Horse Show, led round by our *syce*, and won my very first prize (probably because I was the youngest entrant by a long way). That prize was a huge blue-beribboned box of chocolates – I can see the box and smell and taste the chocolates now . . .

Our return to Dehra Dun was made in The Grumble-Box. A journey of more than 1800 miles, mostly over quite roughly surfaced dusty roads, this was quite a feat. Mummy was seven months pregnant at the time, so it must have been an uncomfortable journey for her – but it was great fun for me. The old car performed valiantly and we arrived at our next Dehra Dun house, 7 Ghangora, in October. On the 22nd December, my sister Caroline was born in the Coronation Hospital in Dehra Dun.

My memories of Dehra are rather scattered and jumbly, but what I do remember, I remember vividly. I was forbidden to go into the 'jungle' behind our bungalow 'because there are snakes and tigers'. I had a pet faun – or perhaps it was a goat – and one day she broke loose from her tether and I thought she was lost. I looked for her everywhere, finally braving 'the jungle' alone. It was a terrible disappointment. I saw not a single tiger. Met not a single snake. And I did not find my pet. No doubt she *did* meet a tiger in the jungle. I just got a beating for being naughty and disobedient. I was already being naughty and disobedient. Always getting beatings.

Best of all my memories are those of picnics. Regular events. My favourite spot was by the Doon, a wide but quite shallow river that flowed over and in between huge dappled and rounded boulders, stones and pebbles, with sandy little beaches here and there for digging in and playing games. How I loved that river. It must have been then that I discovered that rivers were special, and the tumbling water thrilled and exhilarated me. Silvery-leaved trees rustled and sunburnt grasses fluttered in the breeze as we enjoyed our leisurely picnics, spread on gigantic flat stones, smoothed by their violent journeys down from the mountains when the rivers came into spate. There are photographs of such picnics in the family albums. Of myself standing in the ice-clear water, wearing my white solar topee [pith helmet] to protect me from the sun. I was a pretty little girl then. Small and dainty. But already rebellious. Resisting my mother's authority. Annoyed by her attempts to discipline me and impose her will.

I adored my father. He taught me to love steam engines and model railways. He had his own unique and intricately pointed 'O' gauge railway layout on the verandah of the bungalow. Signals and sidings. One very special engine was powered by real steam! He kept the secret of how the steam was produced until I squeezed the explanation from him. A proper boiler, water-filled and heated by a real fire fuelled by methylated spirits. Puff, puff, puff the engine went – and faster and faster, rattling over the points at dare-devil speed. Seldom, but sometimes, we'd have a derailment. That was very exciting and I'd clap my hands. Some of the coaches Daddy had made himself. A dining car's the one I remember best – with wooden table and seats, curtains at the windows and tiny table lamps. Daddy's railway was a masterpiece then, and he added to and improved it as the years went by. Alas, after his death in 1969 the entire collection was sold. Every single truck and rail. When I was told that it had gone, dismantled, packed up and taken away who knows where, I burst into tears. It was the end of an era. Daddy's trains. A reminder of the cruel passing of time. A brutal blow. But I have one favourite picture to remind me of our mutual love. Terence Cuneo's *Lickey Incline*. A print my mother never allowed Daddy to frame and hang (because our cottage was too small). She gave it to me after my father died, still rolled in its card-board tube. Now it is grandly framed and hangs prominently in my cottage.

After every railway journey, back 'home' and frequently travel-ling between London and Glasgow, my father would always take me along the platform to thank the engine driver for my safe journey. Really, it was Daddy's excuse to start up a conversation with the driver and fireman and to inspect the cab!

More of my father later. India again. When I was four years old I became dreadfully ill with septicaemia, pneumonia and even cardiac failure. The doctors, afterwards, summarised it in a letter (see next page). I was in bed for more than two months and on the 'danger-ously ill' list for fourteen days. Day nurses and night nurses cared for me. My temperature soared to 105°F. I suffered awful indignities

JANE DONALDSON

C.I.M.Hospital, Dehra Dun, U.P.,

India, March 16th, 1937.

Dear Doctor:

Following is a report on the illness of Miss Jane Auld:

During October, 1936, she developed an acute upper respiratory infection, streptococcal in origin. It involved the sinuses, antra, naso-pharynx and pharynx extensively. On the fifth day of her illness she developed an acute myocardial failure. Following this her condition became very low but after some difficulty she responded to treatment. Anti-streptococcal serum along with stimulants were administered. On the tenth day a large swelling involved the central part of the forehead and extended down to the angle of the right eye. As it obviously contained puss it was opened in two places, once over the forehead and a counter opening near the angle of the eye. About one ounce of puss was evacuated. From this time on the patient's progress was very slow and the temperature did not finally settle down until the 50th day. Since then the wound has broken down periodically and discharged small amounts of serous fluid. On the last occasion a small piece of hard bony-like matter was extracted. It measured 2 cm. by 2 mm. by 1 mm.

The heart condition has cleared up completely. X-ray taken here showed no evidences of bony involvement. Further investigation is desirable with a view to clearing up the discharge from the old scars. It was not considered advisable to proceed further in this matter here on account of local climatic conditions.

Yours sincerely,

(Capt. W. J. Virgin, I.M.S.)

P.S. I am enclosing the patient's temperature chart and request that you will return it to the parents when you are finished with it.

14

like enemas, 'turpentine stoops' and copious dosings of castor oil. My breathing became so bad that steam kettles and Friars Balsam inhalations were necessary. I even had to swallow one and a half ounces of brandy each day. Fortunately a young, newly qualified Canadian army doctor by the name of Captain Virgin arrived on the scene. He risked the use of a new German drug called Prontosyl before he had any experience of it and without knowing what dose he should administer. But it worked, and I took a turn for the better almost at once. Nevertheless, it was a long and tedious convalescence trying to build up my strength for the steamship journey back to England. I had a horrible septic wound in my forehead that required painful daily dressings and the constant wearing of a head bandage to keep out infection. It was thought that I had picked up the streptococcal infection in a dirty swimming pool. But everyone tried to keep me amused, and I lay in a lovely day bed on the lawn all day under a shady tree with screens to shield me from the breeze.

When I was strong enough we took ship again for home, this time on the *City of Canterbury*. During the three-week journey, my wound had to be dressed each day to keep it open and prevent the skin healing over before I could be seen by the specialist in Glasgow. But I enjoyed my journey all the same, tossing my topee into the Suez Canal with delight in the traditional manner when the time came.

I had no idea then that I was leaving behind me a country that had been the home of my maternal ancestors since the eighteenth century. I was not to visit India again for nearly fifty years!

Chapter Two

Within the month we were in Scotland, the home of my father's family, the Aulds.

The Aulds were an Ayrshire family of some substance in the seventeenth, eighteenth and nineteenth centuries. Robert Auld, 'Laird of Ellanton'[2], had an estate, Dankeith, between Symington and Dundonald. He must have been born in about 1680 and died around 1750–60. He married one Margaret Campbell, by whom he had two sons, Robert and William[3], and a daughter, Jean (who died in 1759). Robert junior farmed at Underwood, on the Ellanton estate, and he married Christina Knox – a relation of John Knox. William, the second son, remained a bachelor. He went into the Church and became Minister of Mauchline. During his ministry he achieved a place in history because of his vilification of Robert Burns, castigating him for his immorality and his fornication with Jean Armour (who shared my birthday – 27th February). William was immortalised by Burns in a verse of his poem 'The Kirk's Alarm':

> Daddie Auld! Daddie Auld, there's a tod[4] in the fauld,
> A tod meikle[5] waur[6] than the clerk;
> Tho' ye do little skaith[7], ye'll be in at the death,
> For if ye canna bite, ye may bark,
> Daddy Auld! Gif ye canna bite, ye may bark.

---

[2] Now Helenton. [3] 1709–91. [4] fox. [5] much. [6] worse. [7] damage.

Robert and Christina Knox Auld had a son, another Robert, born in 1773. Robert was educated at Glasgow and Leyden universities and he also took holy orders. As the Rev. Dr Auld, he became Minister of the Auld Kirk in Ayr in 1800, after the local dignitaries had petitioned the town and parish of Ayr in 1799 that he should be so appointed. Among the signatures on the petition document is one 'Burns' – probably Robert Burns's brother, as the poet had died in 1796. Robert Auld had inherited the Elizabethan mansion at Dankeith from his grandfather and lived there until, after many struggles with the powers that be within the Church, he was provided with a manse in the town of Ayr. He was awarded the Freedom of the City of Ayr in 1802 and of Glasgow in 1839. I have the fine portrait of him by Graham Gilbert, probably painted at about that time. He had married Susannah Alexis Wilson in 1801, daughter of the Rev. John Wilson, Minister of Neilston, near Glasgow (who had been given the Freedom of the City of Paisley in 1768 – I have the document granting this, on parchment). Robert and his wife Susannah had a large family – four sons and five daughters (see family tree).

William Auld, named after his Great Uncle 'Daddy' Auld, was one of the youngest of the family, born in 1814. He, however, was not ecclesiastically inclined and became a successful accountant and stockbroker. He was, indeed, one of the founder members in 1844 of the Glasgow Stock Exchange. William married twice. His first wife, Connel Simpson, died aged 45 in 1853 after having borne him six children, one of whom, Christina Knox Auld, died when she was a baby. I have her memorial ring, entwined with her hair and inscribed 'Christina Knox Auld died 1850 aged 16 months'. By his second wife, Isabella, he sired three daughters and a son, my grandfather, William Auld, born in 1868.

It was Great Grandfather William Auld who purchased the family table silver in 1838 – a magnificent canteen of twenty-four Queen's pattern (Queen Victoria had come to the throne the previous year) place settings which is still almost intact. That table silver has been used by our family for nearly 200 years and it is very special to us.

JANE DONALDSON

THE AULD FAMILY TREE

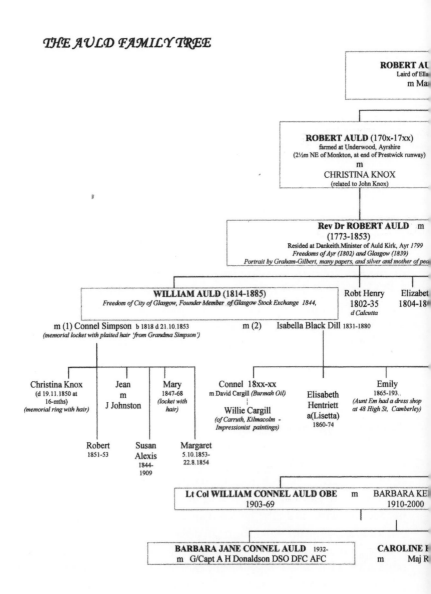

Oct 2003/auldtree.doc

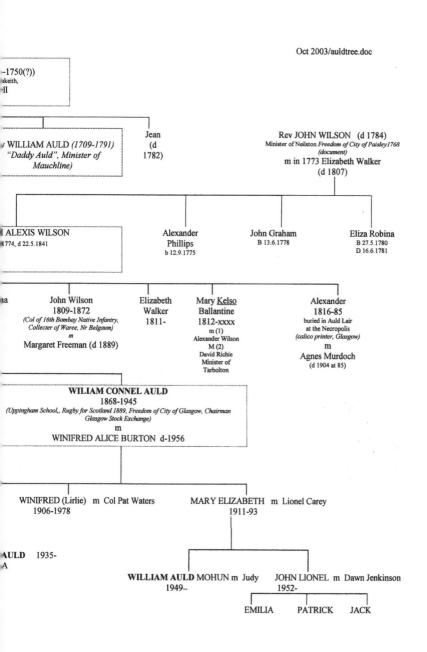

−1750(?))
akeith,
II

WILLIAM AULD *(1709-1791)*
"Daddy Auld", Minister of
Mauchline)

Jean
(d
1782)

Rev JOHN WILSON (d 1784)
Minister of Neilston *Freedom of City of Paisley 1768*
(document)
m in 1773 Elizabeth Walker
(d 1807)

ALEXIS WILSON
774, d 22.5.1841

Alexander
Phillips
b 12.9.1775

John Graham
B 13.6.1778

Eliza Robina
B 27.5.1780
D 16.6.1781

na

John Wilson
1809-1872
(Col of 16th Bombay Native Infantry,
Collecter of Waree, Nr Belgaum)
m
Margaret Freeman (d 1889)

Elizabeth
Walker
1811-

Mary Kelso
Ballantine
1812-xxxx
m (1)
Alexander Wilson
M (2)
David Richie
Minister of
Tarbolton

Alexander
1816-85
buried in Auld Lair
at the Necropolis
(calico printer, Glasgow)
m
Agnes Murdoch
(d 1904 at 85)

WILIAM CONNEL AULD
1868-1945
(Uppingham School,, Rugby for Scotland 1889, Freedom of City of Glasgow, Chairman
Glasgow Stock Exchange)
m
WINIFRED ALICE BURTON d-1956

WINIFRED (Lirlie) m Col Pat Waters
1906-1978

MARY ELIZABETH m Lionel Carey
1911-93

AULD   1935-
A

WILLIAM AULD MOHUN m Judy
1949-

JOHN LIONEL m Dawn Jenkinson
1952-

EMILIA   PATRICK   JACK

19

As I dump my cats' dinners onto their plates with a perfectly balanced silver spoon, I often wonder what my great-grandfather would think of my eccentric and humble cottage and our chaotic late twentieth/early twenty-first century lifestyles – the contrast with his grand town house at Park Terrace in Glasgow and his Victorian well-ordered prosperity would be quite a shock to him.

My grandfather was born on the 25th April 1868 and educated at Uppingham, where he excelled himself at rugby. Later, in 1889, he played for Scotland, and he also captained the West of Scotland, earning caps that we still treasure (these, and one of his Scotland jerseys, are now in the Scottish RFU Museum at Murrayfield). He became a stockbroker and chartered accountant and commuted daily by train to the city of Glasgow from what was in those days a small village, Kilmacolm in Renfrewshire. His sister Connel Cargill and her husband David Syme Cargill (he of Burmah Oil) lived quite close at Carruth (near which they founded a home for orphans). It was in Kilmacolm that he met and fell in love with Winnie, a young schoolmistress at St Columba's School.

Winifred Burton was something of a rarity in those days: an extremely attractive woman who was also well educated and was following a professional career. Born in Norwich, she was the second in a family of five children, who early in life suffered a severe family trauma. The story goes that their grandfather, James Clark, was the chief accountant of the Norwich Union Insurance Company. Unfortunately he is said to have abused his position and milked a considerable amount of money from his employers over a period of years. The time came when he realised that he had been found out and was about to be brought to justice. Fearful of the shame he knew would ensue he decided to shoot himself, leaving his poor wife to bring up their family alone.

James Clark had six children, five daughters and one son. His youngest daughter, Alice, was apparently a great beauty. She married Robert Gent Burton, of the brewery family, by whom she bore Harold, Louis, Winifred, Alice, Mabel and Lillian – known as Jessican.

Winnie and her sisters, Alice, Mabel and Jessican, were brought up by their two maiden aunts, James's daughters, who ran a school for young ladies and had very advanced ideas about young women's education. The school was housed in an historic sixteenth-century building with a later Georgian front in the centre of Norwich known as Surrey House, in Surrey Street. The house is now long gone, and on that ground has arisen the new modern headquarters of the Norwich Union Insurance Company, no less! Norwich Union (now Aviva) have 'Surrey House, Surrey Street' as part of their address. The old Surrey House had a large walled garden and an orchard, and the three sisters enjoyed a happy childhood with the benefit of a first-class education. Later, Winnie attended college in London to train as a schoolmistress, and her first post had taken her to Kilmacolm. Here she met and fell in love with William Auld, by then a junior partner in a Glasgow firm of chartered accountants.

Once William and Winnie had married they settled in a house called Glenfinnart, in Kilmacolm, where on the 26th November 1903 my father William Connel Auld (always known as Billy) was born. He was followed by two daughters, Lirlie and Mary, and soon the family moved to a larger house, Larchmont, on the Bridge-of-Weir road.

My grandfather prospered as a chartered accountant, although his career was interrupted by four years' service in the Highland Light Infantry during The Great War. When the war was over, the family moved to a much larger and grander house, The Grange, in Bridge-of-Weir. Originally a tannery village, Bridge-of-Weir had by then, like Kilmacolm, become popular with commuters, with its excellent train service to Glasgow, and there were many substantial houses being built on the hill to the south of the River Weir, as well as two excellent golf courses.

Billy went to the prep school for Rugby and was later sent to Glenalmond (known as the Eton of Scotland) in the foothills of the Highlands, near Crieff. He had actually won a scholarship to Rugby, but when The Great War began it was decided he should be educated nearer to home. He was a clever boy and good at games, playing rugby for the school, and he was an excellent shot. He was practical, too, always making or mending things and tinkering with his motorbike. He decided on a career in the army, and after leaving school he attended the Royal Military Academy at Woolwich. He had, in fact, passed the entrance exam to Sandhurst (supposedly more difficult in those days), but he was intent upon becoming a gunner rather than an engineer. After passing out of Woolwich he was posted to a Mountain Battery of the Royal Artillery on the North West Frontier of India – which was right up his street.

Life on the North West Frontier was dangerous. There were continuous scuffles over the Afghanistan border and rebellious native tribes to control. Communication was hazardous. There were no made-up roads and the field guns and equipment had to be transported by mule trains along steep and rocky mountain tracks. My father adored this life in the mountains. There was shooting and mountaineering and polo, combined with the close camaraderie of a regiment who spent many months at a time away from civilisation.

My Keelan grandfather was then General Manager of the East Indian Railway, based in Lucknow. He lived in an apartment in the former Chutter Munzl Palace, on the banks of the Jumna river. The British had converted the former palace into the Chutter Munzl Club, where there were tennis courts, a swimming pool and beautiful gardens. 'Buddha', as we called my grandfather, was the Honorary Secretary of the Club, hence the grace-and-favour apartment overlooking the river. Dances were held regularly in the pillared ballroom (reputed to have the finest sprung dance floor in India), and it was at one of these that Barbara Keelan was introduced to Captain William Auld, RA.

For Billy it was love at first sight, but Barbara was reluctant to be wooed by him. She had a bevy of other admirers who seemed more dashing than the rather solid, Scottish Billy. But his persistence was eventually rewarded, and in November 1930 they were married in Calcutta Cathedral, with my Aunt Pamela acting as bridesmaid.

So, when I was brought back to Scotland it was to be introduced to the long, long association of the Auld family with Ayrshire and Glasgow – but it was not until nearly sixty years later that I began seriously to unravel the family threads and discover the ancestors of which I am now so proud.

Calcutta Cathedral, 26th November 1930.

Chapter Three

Soon after we arrived in Bridge-of-Weir, I was taken to a nursing home in Glasgow and underwent an operation to remove more bits of loose bone from my forehead and to clean up my ugly wound. Once I was convalescent again it was back to Bridge-of-Weir and to lots of fun with Mummy and Daddy. There were also visits to the seaside at St Andrews and to some of our rather grander relations, the Todds at Trochrague and the McCowans on the banks of Loch Lomond, in their big houses, which seemed like castles to me. It was no time before Daddy's leave was over and my parents had to return to India. Obviously I could not go with them, because I still needed treatment and had to keep a dressing on my forehead, so my sister Caroline and I remained at The Grange.

My grandparents were not rich, but they were comfortably off. The house seemed huge to me. It was a typical early twentieth-century Scots gentleman's house, with definite touches of Charles Rennie Macintosh about it, turreted, pebble-dashed and painted white. The front door, set in the angle of an L-shaped frontage, opened into a lobby leading to a large entrance hall. This could be partly curtained off with heavy red-velvet curtains, and in winter there was always a coal fire burning, round which comfortable sofas and armchairs were arranged.

The drawing room was furnished in soft shades of beige and

powder-blue. There was a large bow window with a cushioned window seat where one could sit and enjoy the vista of Granny's garden and the splendid open views towards the loch and hills beyond. There was a grand piano, on which Granny would play for hours on end with me rapt beside her, the two of us singing together all her favourite songs – 'Keep the Home Fires Burning', 'There's a Long Long Trail Awinding', 'It's a Long Way to Tipperary', 'Pack up Your Troubles in Your Old Kit Bag', 'If You Were the Only Girl in the World'. I still remember most of the words off by heart.

The Grange had a way of life and an orderliness that seem completely remote from today's world. It was 'polished'. The furniture shone from daily dusting. Silver, brass and copper always gleamed. Linen was scrubbed, starched and ironed by hand in the laundry-room. There were fresh flowers in all the rooms. Fireplaces were cleaned out each morning and new fires were laid ready to be lit when the time came. It was a well-mannered, happy house in which to live.

Meals were quite formal affairs, always punctually served in the dining room ten minutes after the first of two gongs had been sounded. A maid wearing a black dress and starched organdie cap and apron would help Gag-Gag by handing round the food after he had carved and clearing away the plates between serving further courses.

Beyond the green baize door by the foot of the main staircase was another world. A cosy day nursery where we could play on rainy days while Nanny sat and sewed. The butler's pantry where glasses, silver, cutlery and plates were washed, polished and put away in glass-fronted cupboards and baize-lined drawers. It was always called 'the butler's pantry' – although there was no butler! Then came the kitchen, with a black iron range, a deep china sink and Dutch airers suspended from the ceiling. A scrubbed wooden table was by the window, and heavy black iron cooking pots were stacked on shelves. Down the passage were the larder, the laundry-room, the coal store and 'Billy's Workshop'. This was where my father had a workbench and kept all his tools neatly arranged on the wall.

Upstairs, reached by a wide front staircase and a narrow one at the back for the servants and children, were the five main bedrooms and two bathrooms. A narrow corridor led from the top of the back stairs, off which were the night-nursery and maids' bedrooms. A second staircase led up to 'wonderland' – the billiard room. This was paradise for children. It was stuffed with stored furniture and knick-knacks, china and carpets for which there was no room in the house. Attics led off this room, all with boarded floors and, because of the unusual shape of the house, all twisty and intriguing. In the attics were chests full of dressing-up clothes. Shawls, hats, dresses, fans, furs. There was even a whole *bearskin*, with a stuffed head. He was a very moth-eaten bear by then. I still have two of the shawls. One red with cream embroidery, the other purple with crimson and shocking pink roses and long fringes.

The Grange had a large lawn and a shrubbery. An Alpine garden bordered the south side of the house and there was a rose garden, a vegetable garden, a tennis court – and an exciting wood as well. In the nursery there were nannies. A succession of them. None would stay for long because I was so naughty. But one, Nanny Molly, persevered and understood me – and I grew to love her. Both she and Granny wrote long letters to my parents in India to help them not to miss us too much.

Extracts from letters to my parents in India whilst we were left with our Auld grandparents at The Grange

I am making enquiries about reading lessons for her. Mary Stephens has gone away for a fortnight, but Jean Gow is asking her governess if she could take her with Jock from 9.30 till 11 each day. I think she'd be the better of definite occupation.

Jane never forgets her. She always talks of Mummy every day, and if she is nice to Carol at once Mummy must be told! She is better – but still announces she's going to cut off her head or drown her at intervals. Her prayers are a source of great interest and she would like to boss the Almighty as she tries to boss everyone else. I assured her the other day that God expected her to do as she was told but did not expect her to tell him what to do. "How can he do what I want if I don't tell him to do it?"

She has to amuse herself quite a lot. The thing I find most difficult to combat is the fact that she won't do anything "at once" – there's always argument and putting off. She's "agin the Government". No sooner is she told to do something than that is the one thing she doesn't want to do – especially if she's wanted to hurry over it!

Jane sang to her and said a piece of poetry out of Christopher Robin.

Jane as brown and freckled as possible and Carol rosy and gay and disgracefully rowdy! Carol makes friends with everyone on the shore – but Jane is more particular!

We took Jane to St Leonards on Saturday, to watch Mary play cricket, and she was very funny and amused Miss Pridden and the girls by her very apt comments.

Jane is the cutest, wiliest little monkey, but she's such fun and a delightful companion – one of the most intelligent children I know.

Jane goes about with Barbara's letter always and is able to read some bits of it – she's always asking what the words spell. Nanny forgot to pack yours and Barbara's photograph and Jane was very sad – but the letter has to be kissed nightly. There is absolutely no fear of her forgetting you – never a day passes that she does not have a talk or write a letter to Mummy or Daddy. In her prayers she always says "Mummy and Daddy must come first" – but I regret to say she sometimes continues "Carol will come last"!! which always brings forth a lecture from Granny, without the slightest impression!

Jane has just come in with a lovely bowl of flowers for me – she cut them all herself, chose the bowl and arranged them – so nicely – "2 Sweet Williams – one for Gag-Gag and one for Daddy – and one rose, the prettiest, for Mummy".

Jane went right in to the water, copying the commonest child I ever saw – who was sweet to her! Jane is splendid at running errands for us now – good as gold. In some ways she has improved enormously and sometimes she is beginning to be very sweet to Carol – but another time she is the old demon and says the horridest things. She is an amazingly intelligent child. I came by train with her yesterday and she noticed everything and knew far more about the trains and signals and lines etc than I did. The Forth Bridge was a huge joy to her.

Letter from Nanny to Mummy and Daddy

The King and Queen were in Glasgow on Friday and Jane went up to see them from Mr Auld's office. She was thrilled. Her only disappointment was that the Princesses weren't there; she takes a tremendous interest in them.

. . . back to Granny

Jane was delighted with your letter, which she tries to read in bed. She is devoted to you really and whenever I tell her she's been a good girl and kind to Carol she always says "will you write and tell Mummy", and if I give her a scolding and tell her how horrid she has been and how nice Carol was to her she always says, when she recovers herself – "you won't write to Mummy about it, will you?". I told her yesterday that I would tell you she had been kind to Carol for a whole day. Jane is being very good about running messages now – helps me with my flowers always and helps Marion tidy and carry.

We came home to a tremendous welcome from both of them, and Jessican says that after she smacked Jane's hand once she had no further trouble with her. Certainly she is improving and is really much better with Carol. She's lost her lovely colour from St Andrews, which is very sad, and she's growing very tall – not putting on any weight, she's just 3 stone and 1lb now.

She always wants you and Daddy when she goes to bed – but she doesn't cry now, because she wants me "to tell Mummy how good she is". She kisses your photograph even when she wakes up in the night.

Oh! The cuteness of her. On Monday morning she was horrid – and how she tried to wangle me all that day! I said she might come in beside me and chalk or do a puzzle, but I would not play. Well, she tried by hook or crook to turn everything into a game. "I'll be Princess Elizabeth drawing and you're Queen Elizabeth making me a frock" etc etc. The ingenuity of her. "I'm Princess Elizabeth tidying up after Princess Margaret Rose and you'll say 'What a nice little girl Elizabeth is today'"! Marvellous!

I loved The Grange. I adored my grandmother. I was very, very happy. My Grandfather Gag-Gag I loved too, of course, but I was always a little in awe of him, and he used to pretend to be strict with little girls (he wasn't a bit strict really). I hated my sister. Because she was always so good, because she had always been spoilt by Mummy and because she was fat and cuddly – not skinny like me – and everyone used to say how sweet she was.

During our stay I had to have my tonsils out. One did not go to hospital for such an operation in those days. The doctors came to the house. A temporary 'operating theatre' was set up in the kitchen. A surgeon came from Glasgow and the local GP, Dr Peebles-Brown, clamped a chloroform (more likely ether) pad over my face to anaesthetise me. I lay on an ironing board while my tonsils were snipped out, suffering no ill effects thereafter.

Sept 7, 4pm, The Grange
Well, the wee lass had the operation this morning. She is pretty miserable at the moment, but has slept off and on since it was done. Dr Harper came at 9.45 and was just 10 minutes doing it. Said they were very 'mucky'. She was <u>awfully</u> good, dear wee mite.

The wee soul has had another rather miserable day – she won't swallow and won't talk – but Dr Peebles-Brown is quite pleased with her. She has eaten about 3 spoonfuls of porridge, some ice cream, 2 spoonfuls of chicken jelly, 2 cups of tea and 2 glasses of lemon barley water with glucose. Grapes, plums, pears, chicken cream, whipped egg – all were scorned, and the doctor said we needn't force her to eat today, so we didn't. She's had two good sleeps today and was asleep by 8 tonight, so I hope she'll be much better tomorrow.

She has spent the day opening parcels. Gag-Gag gave her a doll she loves – a washable baby – and it has never left her arms. The Todds sent her grapes. I had a book posted to her, and a basket of all different fruits. Jessican sent her books and a scrapbook. Marion brought her a lovely musical toy and a book, and gave Carol a cutting-out book to give her.

Mary sent her a book, Snakes and Ladders and a cutting-out thing of the Coronation, and Elma Scott a jigsaw puzzle – so the wee dear was very important. She couldn't be bothered with toys today, but loved getting the parcels, and she has been read to all day by someone or other, just to keep her quiet. She is very sweet and good and should be much better tomorrow.

A frequent visitor to The Grange was my father's younger sister, Mary. 'Uncle Mary' I used to call her, because she was a real tomboy and she smoked a pipe and rode a motorbike – which I thought were magnificent things for an aunt to do. She also adored dogs. There were two in the house. Laddie, a dear old black labrador, and Jill (Mary's own dog), a wire-haired terrier. Jill had puppies while we were there, and they lived in a wonderful kennel-house in the garden. It was a large kennel with a cosy little bedroom at one end and a railed roofed-in run at the other. The puppies could jump up onto the wide shelf above the 'bedroom' and play chasing games. I would spend hours in the kennel with them, pretending I was a puppy too.

Mary had attended St Leonard's School in St Andrews and then joined the FANY (First Aid Nursing Yeomanry) and was in charge of her unit in Camberley when Princess Elizabeth was posted there to be taught to drive and to learn about the mechanical innards of army cars and lorries. Mary personally taught her the latter subject – we have a photograph of the team with Mary and the Princess sitting in the front row with Mary's dog, a Sheltie, sitting spread across both their laps. Mary was married towards the end of the war to Lionel Carey, a housemaster at Christ's Hospital at Horsham. I was a bridesmaid at the wedding, together with two Carey girls. This marriage forged especially strong links with the Carey family that still endure to this day.

Many are the memories of life at The Grange. The special smell of the granite gravel on a damp morning. The funny telephone in the hall with the mouthpiece mounted on the wall and the earpiece on the end of a long flex. The huge garage for two cars. The twin weeping elms on the lawn (which, sadly, in the 1970s and 1980s both fell victim to Dutch Elm Disease), behind whose drooping fronds one could hide from Nanny. The dark-green revolving summer-house where we would have elevenses and afternoon tea on sunny days, and dolls' parties with nasturtium-leaf sandwiches. The tennis court and the wood beyond. Granny's Alpine garden, with its twisty stone path and cushions of unusual flowers, heathers and shrubs and rustic seats and benches. Gentians, gentians, gentians – intensely blue and Granny's favourite flower.

All too soon, it seemed, this part of my life came to an end. My parents came back from India, and the nomadic life of an army family began.

Daddy as Mr McGregor chasing me (Peter Rabbit) with a long rake.

Chapter Four

Daddy's first posting in England was to the Royal Artillery Depot at Woolwich, in South East London. It was a short posting and we rented a semi-detached, two-storey villa in a rather dismal road in Blackheath. It was winter, and the tiny piece of 'garden' in front of the house was brown and desolate-looking. The short path up to the front door had chipped red, brown and blue mosaic tiles and the entrance was dark and forbidding. Inside, too, the house seemed dark and dismal.

Christmas that year was the first real Christmas that I can remember – with stockings at the end of the bed and a Christmas tree with lights. The anticipation was almost frightening and the joy unbearable when I opened the parcel containing my beautiful new doll with shutting eyes – Belinda Blue-Eyes. Although it was a dark and poky house we had a wonderful Christmas. My nanny of the time told me an incredible tale about her mother having a black cat that was almost human. It would go to the lavatory like a real person, straddling its legs over the seat!

Our next move was to Ash Vale, while Daddy attended the Staff College at nearby Camberley. We took a furnished house called Pine Glen at the fringe of the village. I remember it had a huge pampas grass plant growing close to the garage, which would scratch you horribly as you passed. Pine Glen was a hideous house, probably built in the 1920s, with a very dark kitchen. Poor Mummy, who had never had to cook before, had to learn in that kitchen. Everything was dark green and cream, including the 'Judge' enamel saucepans.

Nevertheless, the house was good for children – or rather the surroundings were. It was approached from the village by a stretch of sandy private road leading to heathland, where we could walk and play 'let's pretend'. There was the canal nearby where we could fish and watch the ducks and swans with their cygnets and ride our bikes along the towpath. There were trips on summer weekends to Mytchett Lido, which I thought was a most glamorous place – a large lake within pine woods surrounded by a sandy beach, with facilities for swimming and diving. Nanny always called it Mytchett 'Lie-dough', of which my parents did not approve – so I called it 'Lie-dough' too!

One day, visiting Buddhi and Buddha, my Keelan grandparents, who were staying in an hotel in Camberley, I tried to drown my sister Carol. She was, as usual, being annoying. I pushed her into a lily pond in the hotel garden, hoping it was full of frogs and telling everyone that I wanted to murder her.

It was at Ash Vale that I first remember meeting my mother's sister, Pamela. She must have been about seventeen then, and I thought her quite beautiful. She had enormous blue eyes and she sat in a deck chair in the garden in front of a herbaceous border of delphiniums and lupins in every shade of blue, making a lovely and indelible picture.

Once there was a fire on the heath, and fire engines, bells ringing frantically, clanged past the house to put it out. All the children ran chasing the fire engines and stood by, spellbound, as the firemen fought the flames.

I had been taught to read and write by a governess at the house of the Gows, friends of Granny's near Bridge-of-Weir, whose son Jock was about my age, but now I was sent to Miss Seed's school in Aldershot. By coincidence they had a fire there too during one of the holidays. We all went back to school late the following term because the repairs had not been finished in time. It was at Miss Seed's that I made my first, and last, stage appearance, as Mustard

Seed in *As You Like It*. I still have the programme with my name JANE AULD printed on it. I have my very first school reports from here, too. Indeed, I have all my school reports – and worse and worse they were to get.

Then came the threat of war, and Daddy was unable to complete his course at the Staff College because he was posted to Larkhill, on Salisbury Plain, as an instructor in gunnery. We moved to a pretty thatched cottage in Amesbury – Barn Cottage. I recall being punished there by being locked in my bedroom by Nanny for several hours (probably for being horrible to my sister). I remember dying to pee and screaming to be let out. Nasty Nanny paid no attention, so I tipped the water out of my bedside carafe, peed into it and then lay in wait for Nanny to pass below the window, which eventually she did. I then tipped the contents of the carafe onto her head, all the while half screaming in anger, half screeching with laughter.

There are more placid memories of Amesbury too. Summer picnics and walks through the water meadows by the River Avon, waist-high in grasses and buttercups, wearing smocked Liberty dresses and straw hats decorated with poppies, cornflowers and daisies. I was a neat and well-proportioned child, though I did not realise it then. My legs were long and the right shape. Daddy used to call me his 'skinny-me-linka-long-legs-with-pink-banana-feet'. But my poor little face was marred by my dreadful scar, of which I was, fortunately, never conscious. It never gave me any hang-ups, as scars are supposed to do. I simply did not notice it. I did not see it when I looked at myself in the mirror, which I did frequently. Not, as everyone thought, because I was vain, but because I was so self-conscious. I hated my thin wormy pigtails, my stick-like arms. They must be so ugly, I thought. Everyone always went on and on about my sister Carol. 'What a *good* girl'. 'What a sweet little fatty'. 'Pudge', Daddy and Mummy called her. How I longed to be fat.

After about six months, we were given an army quarter at Larkhill: 5 Fargo Road. I was sent to Avondale School, Amesbury, or 'Captain Perks's' as it was known. Captain Perks was a stern headmaster, and he seemed dreadfully old and shabby. The classroom on the first floor was gloomy and Victorian in atmosphere – and 'Perky-Boy' was a Victorian disciplinarian. We had to write in old-fashioned copperplate hand, and our knuckles were rapped with his ruler if we wrote carelessly, made blots or spelt badly. Nevertheless, we were given a very good grounding in the three 'R's. The smell of over-cooked beef, blackened and soggy roast potatoes and wishy-washy cabbage still assails my nostrils as I negotiate the roundabout on the Amesbury bypass and see out of the corner of my eye the staddlestones by the front door of Avondale. I am always taken back in time to the lean-to dining room at the back of the house where our midday meals were served.

Shortly after settling in to 5 Fargo Road, I discovered that the taste of alcohol and the whiff of a cigarette were quite delicious. When my parents had been entertaining friends, I would go round the room sipping up all the dregs from the glasses and lighting up the fag-ends for a puff. This made me feel very grown-up. One day Mummy asked, 'Would you like to try a proper cigarette darling?' '*Yes please!*' said seven-year-old I. I was duly allowed to light one up and I quite enjoyed the first few puffs. Determined to pretend that I was continuing to enjoy myself, I persevered smilingly until I had finished the whole cigarette. 'Would you like another?' said Mummy. 'Yes please. . .' I think I managed about one and a half cigarettes before the most terrible wave of nausea overcame me and my head began to spin. I had to be carried upstairs, where I was violently sick and put to bed for twenty-four hours. Mummy told me I turned nearly as green as a pea just before I gave up the pretence of enjoyment. It was several years before I was again tempted by the weed. But tempted eventually I was.

In the August of 1939, we spent a holiday at Bigbury-on-Sea in Devonshire. In those days this was just a small seaside village with a wonderful expanse of sandy beach bordered with rocks and rocky pools. A few hundred yards from the cliff, across the water, is tiny Burgh Island, on which there is a very stylish Art Deco, white stucco hotel, supposed to have been the setting for Agatha Christie's

Ten Little Niggers. At low tide one could walk or even drive a car across the sand to the island, but when the tide was in, a tractor-like construction on stilts, with enormous rubber wheels, would plough its way to and from the mainland through the water, which only ever reached a few feet in depth.

We had taken a small wooden chalet-style bungalow for a couple of weeks. It had rampant honeysuckle all over the front porch and the scent was very strong – a sniff of honeysuckle always reminds me of that summer in Bigbury. I would get up very early each morning and enjoy the expanse of miles of freshly washed sand – the tide always seemed to be out! Behind the island the sea was a sparkly blue and the sky above always seemed to be cloudless. I don't think we had one rainy day. We spent our time on the beach, paddling, shrimping, picnicking and playing in the rock pools or burying each other in the sand.

Hardly had we unpacked after our holiday when, on September 3rd, war was declared – heralding the beginning of a downward plunge in the social history of this country. My father's regiment was quite quickly sent to France, which meant that we lost our married quarter at Larkhill and had nowhere to live. While we had been at Ash Vale my parents had made friends with Rita and James Palmer (James was an instructor at the Staff College in Camberley), and as James, too, had been posted away, Rita offered us a tempo-rary home in her house on the outskirts of Fleet in Hampshire while Mummy looked for somewhere to live. Eventually she found a first-floor flat above a terrace of shops in the main street of Fleet. Mummy, Nanny, my sister and I settled in during the middle of that notoriously cold winter of 1939. All the pipes froze and long fat icicles hung from every drainpipe and roof. Even the leaves on the trees and hedges were covered with a thin film of ice, and we slipped and slithered our way to St Nicholas School each day. We'd take chocolate wafer biscuits to eat with our elevenses – but we'd usually eaten them before we even reached the school gates.

I can remember hearing bands playing and seeing troops marching along Fleet high street, singing stirring marching songs. It was all new and exciting to have a war on, when one did not appreciate what war really meant. Often we marched alongside the soldiers.

Having no garden at the flat, we spent a lot of time at Rita Palmer's house. Copper Beech had a large garden, and only a few hundred yards further down the unmade-up private road were pinewoods and countryside. Rita had a daughter, Cynthia, who was a little younger than I but very nearly as naughty and rebellious. She and I became firm partners in crime and got up to all sorts of mischief together. My sister Carol would always want to tag along with us, which we found very tiresome because she cramped our style. Cynthia and I would disappear for hours together, walking or biking along the towpath of the canal or exploring the woods.

One day we ventured deep into the pinewoods, this time with Carol tagging along behind. We went further than we'd been before and found ourselves on the marshy fringe of what was obviously a sewage farm. The terrain became boggier and boggier and smellier and smellier. As we progressed we had to jump from tussock to tussock over slimy ordure. The tussocks grew further and further apart and it became more and more difficult for Carol, on her stocky little legs, to keep up with us. But she was determined not to be left behind. We thought this was great sport and egged her on to make bigger and bigger jumps. Inevitably she made one jump too many and missed her footing, falling headlong into the foul-smelling marsh. Howling with laughter at the sight of my poor sister covered in black filth, we pulled her out and headed for home. As we trudged back we realised that there would be hell to pay when we delivered the bedraggled and smelly Carol home. Sure enough, there were thrashings for both of us and a good deep disinfectant bath for Carol.

After France fell, Daddy returned to Larkhill again as an instructor in gunnery and we were given a brand new quarter, 20 Fargo Road. The house faced south towards Amesbury, across corn-fields and pasture in which were clumps of ancient beech trees – planted, it was said, to represent the positions of the British fleet at the Battle of Trafalgar. After the evacuation of Dunkirk, Larkhill was the scene of frenzied activity as our defeated troops began to return. The camp was a staging post for the exhausted and beaten men on the journey back to their regimental bases from the ports. Tents were set up and manned by army wives serving tea and food. My mother was always out making and serving sandwiches and hot drinks to the tired but ever-cheerful men.

Germany was now on the offensive, softening us up for invasion by bombing. Larkhill was on the flight path to Bristol, a prime target, and many a bomb was jettisoned quite close to us by Hun aircraft returning to the Fatherland. Where bombs fell in the chalky fields between Fargo Road and Amesbury, there was a moonscape of white craters and hillocks of thrown-up chalk. We loved to play in these craters and splash in the puddles at the bottom.

One day, a stray bomb fell in a field of cows. News of the event was brought when the batman (Daddy's driver/soldier servant) turned up for work in the morning. I could not wait to inspect the scene, so I saddled my faithful bicycle at once and pedalled furiously along Fargo Road towards Amesbury. What a scene of carnage met my eyes. Dead cows were scattered all over the field. Severed limbs and heads had been tossed hither and thither like flotsam and jetsam. Intestines spewed out of bellies onto the grass. There was blood, flesh and bone everywhere. I was delighted. I thought it was the most amazing sight in the world. A surrealist landscape.

Homeward I rode to fetch my sister and friend Janet, who lived next door, so they too could relish the scene. Rather reluctantly, I thought, they accompanied me back to the field, where the poor little sensitive darlings were terribly upset by the scene that met their eyes. Both wept and were very distressed. Much subdued, we re-mounted our bikes and rode home. Again, I anticipated trouble for me when Mummy found out what I had been up to. Rightly. A beating came my way. I was a horrible bloodthirsty child and I'd purposely upset the younger girls. I was myself disgusting for having enjoyed such a spectacle. Childhood can be a very insensitive time. Soon I would find such a scene quite revolting and deeply distressing – but at that time in my life I was merely fascinated.

Life at Larkhill was super for us children. There were so many of us, and all from similar backgrounds. There must have been thirty officers' quarters in Fargo Road and Strangways, ranging from three-bedroomed captains' houses to grander residences for colonels and the Brigadier. All the younger children went to Captain Perks's School, Avondale. A bus would collect us after breakfast and amble all round the camp picking up passengers. But in the summer we would walk or bicycle down the 'cinder path', the track of an old disused railway line which ran from the back of our quarter across the fields and down to Avondale. In the mornings we'd have to hurry, because we were always late, but in the afternoons we would meander and pick wild flowers or sit under the old hawthorn trees and chatter. Sometimes rival gangs would wage war, setting up ambushes and pouncing on one another.

A lot of the old army huts north of Fargo Road seemed to have been abandoned. They were full of old stationery and broken office furniture. We found ways to break in and we would steal paper and notebooks. The inside walls were covered with obscene graffiti that made us laugh. 'Shit', 'fuck' and the 'C' word. We did not know what they meant but we could guess they were foul and we'd shout them when we wanted to insult each other or the Steel House Kids, the troops' children.

Larkhill was heaven. I had so many friends to play with and so many foes to fight, such as the Steel House Kids, who called us 'filthy officers' twerps'. We'd bicycle past the steel houses screaming vile insults and obscene words as we sped. The soldiers' children would retaliate by shouting insults back and throwing stones at the spokes of our bike wheels, hoping to throw us off. It was like running the gauntlet, and quite frightening – but to achieve it was acknowledged by the rest of the gang as very brave.

Trenches had been dug for the soldiers in which to practice. Some of them were quite complicated in layout, with interlinked passages and corrugated-iron roofs. We would play endless games in them and light fires to keep warm. Daddy could never make out where his precious boxes of Swan Vestas disappeared to. We'd play 'mothers and fathers' too. When I was Mother, Jerome Mostyn would be Father – and we'd be very naughty and play 'I'll show you mine if you'll show me yours', which was all hilarious fun.

There was a plantation of infant fir trees where we'd often play. In that plantation was a big haystack which we'd climb and then dare each other to jump off the top. You can see this plantation now from the Amesbury bypass. The trees are about twenty-feet high!

For a time we had a rich and rather grand neighbour. Mrs Mangle was a most glamorous blonde with a film-star pageboy like Betty Grable's. She was my idol. She had *seventy* pairs of shoes and masses of clothes and furs, boxes full of jewels – and she always reeked of expensive scent. After her came the Grieves. We were told their daughter, Fat Janet (she of the cow-bomb episode), was spoilt. Not forced to eat Captain Perks's filthy cabbage. Not even made to go to school if she didn't feel like it. She would get on the bus and then get off again at the next stop and walk home. Her mother never seemed to chide her.

One day, walking along the cinder path alone, I saw *two real fairies*. I was absolutely *sure*. But my little sister shot me down and told me not to be silly. And the batman, polishing Daddy's boots and buttons, said 'they was prob'ly draggin' flies'.

When Mummy, Daddy and Carol went off for a week to Okehampton, where Daddy had 'practise camp' I was left behind to stay with Major and Mrs Porteous at 4 Strangways. I hated it. Hated it. Their house was horrible. My bedroom was poky. Their nanny was too strict. I was made to go to the lavatory every morning after breakfast. We were never made to do that at home. I *hated* it. What's more, their nanny would always 'look' to make sure I told the truth when I said I'd 'been'. Yuk. It was disgusting.

I fell madly in love with Jerome Mostyn about then. My first love. He taught me how to camouflage myself. In his garden he had a canvas tent (camouflaged, of course). He acquired an old tin bath, filled it with water from the hose and added some secret crystals (permanganate of potash might they have been?). He made me

41

remove all my clothes and immerse myself in the bath and splashed me thoroughly with camouflage-mix. When I emerged I was streaky-brown and dirty looking. Beautifully camouflaged all over. It did not wear off for several weeks.

Happy days. But the time had come when it was felt that I should be sent away to boarding school. To the Royal School for Daughters of Officers in the Army, at Bath. Uniform was purchased. Nametapes were sewn in. Eventually the great day came, and in fear and trepidation I watched my brand new school trunk being loaded into the car. Then we set off for the start of my first term at the Royal School. How many adventures would lie ahead, I wondered?

Chapter Five

I was nine years old when I arrived at the Royal School for Daughters of Officers in the Army in September 1941. In fact, the school was not at Bath, its normal habitat, but at Longleat House, to which it had been evacuated for the duration of the war. I was the smallest and youngest in the school and very nervous when I was introduced to Miss Eleanor Hutchinson, the witch-like housemistress of Newlands, the junior house to which I had been allocated.

Our dormitories were on the second floor at the front of the house, overlooking the drive to Horningsham. There were between five and seven girls in each dormitory, except for the Ten Dorm, situated next door to Bishop Ken's Library on the lakeside corner of the house. Each girl had a black iron bedstead, a chair and a marble-topped chest of drawers with a jug, washbasin and slop-pail.

For some reason Eleanor Hutchinson ('Hutch') took an instant dislike to me. She made no attempt to make me feel at home in her house. She was an evil-featured woman, with greying black hair coiled into a bun at the nape of her scrawny neck, a long pointy nose and spectacles. In those wartime days most women wore their skirts quite short, but Hutch swished about in ankle-length peasanty skirts over taffeta petticoats, which made a crackly rustling as she moved. She always wore the same crêpe-soled Clarks children's sandals with star-shaped cutouts on the instep. You could hear them squeaking as she sneaked about the corridors, eavesdropping for talkers-after-lights.

The Marquess of Bath had generously withdrawn into a suite of only a few rooms on the ground floor of the house, immediately to the west of the entrance hall. The school occupied most of the other rooms, except for the State Apartments and rooms used for the storage of Longleat's own furniture. Even the grand salon was converted into a dormitory accommodating more than twenty beds for more senior girls. All the old masters and the valuable books in the libraries remained in place during the school's occupation, although Bishop Ken's precious library was always kept locked and was only used by the Historical Society. Some beautiful furniture and vases were left in the corridors and in those rooms that were not much used, and it was remarkable that in spite of so many hooligan children tearing about, nothing ever seemed to get damaged.

The two-storey Great Hall on the ground floor was used as our assembly hall for morning and evening prayers and for congregating before we filed into meals. The three rooms used for dining overlooked the lake – the Long Library, the smaller Family Dining Room and the State Dining Room. Rows of long tables were tightly packed in so all the girls and staff could eat their meals together.

Bathrooms were few, and hot water in short supply, so we only bathed once or twice a week – and then sometimes two girls would have to share the same shallow water.

Past Lord Bath's apartment on the ground floor was a suite of rooms used as a sanatorium. I was only confined there once and I did not see 'The Grey Lady'. Other girls swore that they had seen the Longleat ghost, whose figure was reputed to appear and be reflected in the gilded looking glasses in one of these rooms.

We slept, ate and generally lived in Longleat House itself, but to accommodate classrooms a temporary timber building had been constructed to the west of the house, linked to a cellar entrance by a covered way. This was built in the form of a quadrangle surrounding some grass and a single hawthorn tree. Cloakrooms and staff rooms were on the entrance corridor, and the north and south wings contained form rooms, labs and the domestic science kitchen. The western wing housed two more classrooms and the gymnasium.

The stable blocks were used for hobbies and for the sports shop. Longleat had its own hard tennis court, but further grass courts were laid out quite close to the house, as were cricket and lacrosse pitches. Some pitches were further away, on the other side of the lakes.

Lord Bath was indeed a tolerant man to have accepted the invasion of so many exuberant children into his home. He seemed, in fact, to enjoy our company and he soon became a good friend of mine. Frequently, after our high tea, I would tiptoe along to his rooms with some biscuits or cake in my hand and knock on his door. He would let me in and take me to the indoor 'kennel' where Steven, his Great Dane slept. I had made friends with Steven the first moment I met him – thus did my friendship with Lord Bath develop. Because I was so tiny and weighed so little, Steven would let me sit on his back and take me for rides. In return I would save him biscuits from my tea.

I was dreadfully homesick at first, but I soon settled in to boarding school life, although Hutch presented me with a fearsome challenge. She seemed to take a perverted delight in victimising me and she would always punish me for misdemeanours that were not entirely my own, such as talking after lights out. One of her favourite tortures was to confiscate my possessions, often when this was completely unmerited. Torches were not allowed at the school, because of the blackout, but needless to say most of the girls owned them. Mine was discovered and confiscated, but a blind eye was turned on those of other girls. My precious autograph book, too, was confiscated. Once, as a punishment for some minor crime, my wristwatch was taken. At the end of term I would ask for my possessions back – but Hutch would always deny she had them or say she could not find them. Infuriated by this injustice I once crept into her room when I knew she was absent and went through the 'confiscation box'. Sure enough, I found my torch, my tartan-covered autograph book and my watch. I have a very dog-eared letter written to my mother after this discovery that conveys the fury I felt.

Hutch's room had dark green and white ivy-strewn wallpaper. There were dark green velvet curtains at the window and across the alcove that contained her bed. Her room was comfortably furnished with a desk, a couple of armchairs and lots of books (her subject was history). In the winter a coal fire always burned in the grate. It was a cosy room, but I hated it. I hated her.

Some of the punishments she inflicted upon me would, in these more compassionate days, be considered child abuse. One winter night when we had failed to hear the Clarks sandals and crackly petticoats approaching, our dormitory was caught talking after lights out. I had not been soliloquising, but I was in the bed nearest to the door. Hutch vented her fury on me. She grabbed the end of my bed and pulled it out into the corridor, swung it round and dragged me along to the landing at the top of the flight of stairs that led down to the Minstrels' Gallery, then used as the Prefects' Room, overlooking the Great Hall. She boxed in my bed with a couple of screens to make it into a little cell, and then left me there to spend the night. I was made to sleep on this landing for several nights. A more sensitive and less resilient child would have suffered psychological damage or, at the very least, nightmares from such an experience. The eeriness of sleeping in this ghostly place, stared down at by towering portraits of Thynne ancestors and occasionally visited by flapping bats, is impossible to convey. I was quite frightened – but I was determined not to let the hated Hutch know that her punishment had worked. This was the challenge that enabled me to survive unscathed.

The Longleat lavatories were rather special. At least the one on Newland's landing was, and that is the one I remember best. The bowl was patterned with blue and white flowers and it was set in a chest-like construction of solid mahogany, with a heavy mahogany lid. In the top of the chest, to one's right as one sat, was a porcelain and brass handle. Pulling this upwards for several inches flushed the pan with water. This lavatory was almost opposite Hutch's room.

On one occasion I was taken ill during the night. Feeling violently sick and with rumbling tummy pains, I staggered along to the lavatory in my dressing gown. Both stomach and bowels screamed to be emptied at the same time – which is hard to achieve tidily with only one receptacle to hand. Too ill to address such a difficult problem I simply threw up into the pan and let everything else out onto the floor – which was luckily covered with lino. Feeling a little better once I had relieved myself I made the best attempt I could at cleaning up the foul-smelling floor. I managed quite well with the lavatory paper available, but there was inevitably an evil residual pong. I then staggered back to my bed and crashed out.

Next morning a Gestapo-type interrogation took place before breakfast. All the house was summoned to hear what Hutch had to say. 'Nobody is going down to breakfast until I discover the identity of the disgusting girl who fouled the lavatory last night. You will all stand here until the filthy creature owns up!' Embarrassed beyond belief, I had no alternative but to confess, midst the stifled giggles of the other girls. That was *it*. This, to Hutch, was proof positive that I was as evil as she had always thought. No explanations were allowed. In her book I had done the dirty deed on purpose, just to draw attention to myself.

I was in deep trouble. 'Jane Auld is not fit to be spoken to by decent, clean people. She is to be Sent To Coventry immediately. None of you is to speak a single word to her for a whole week. She will sleep on the landing (again!). She will eat her meals at a separate table and she will be isolated in the form room for seven days. Anyone caught speaking to her will be severely punished.' That was that. Back to the spooky landing and to boringly silent meals. My form mistress, whom I quite liked, was made to put my desk under the blackboard, facing outwards towards the rest of the class. Needless to say, ways of communicating with me were found by my friends. Notes were slipped into my desk or cloak pocket, or pushed under my pillow. Faces were pulled in the dining room, and I managed to amuse my classmates by making silly gestures at them from behind the mistresses' backs. So the punishment once again did not really work – although I was greatly relieved when my seven days' isolation was over.

On another occasion, having made one of her frequent accusations that I was dirty (this time my feet and ankles were singled out), I was taken to a bathroom and made to remove my shoes and socks. Hutch then proceeded to attack my heels and ankles with a floor-scrubbing brush, soap and cloudy ammonia. She scrubbed and she scrubbed until my skin was raw and I was yelling before she was satisfied that I was 'clean'.

It is evident from her remarks on my school reports how much she disliked me:

'Jane's behaviour at table is rather uncontrolled. She has a great deal to learn in the House, particularly about being obedient and reliable.'

'Jane has been much less quarrelsome in the dormitory and has stopped pinching and kicking her neighbours at meals. She still has much to learn about being obedient and truthful.'

'Jane must still try to be controlled at table, as well as to be reliable and obedient.'

'There seem to be some signs of improvement about Jane's work. The less said about her conduct at the moment, the better.'

'With regard to others, Jane is unkind, troublesome, impertinent and badly behaved at table. In herself she is untidy, dirty and disobedient. She has been more honest up to half term, but this good sign has now disappeared again.'

'Jane is not quite so untidy and messy as she used to be and during the last fortnight her table manners have improved. It is urgent that she should now cure herself of deliberate deceit in disguising her wrong doings and of defence by half-truths when she is discovered.'

I do not think that woman ever showed me a kindness, but she failed to break me, and in spite of her I had a great deal of fun at Longleat and was very happy.

Our fun was simple. We'd make 'hides' in the twisting branches of the rhododendron bushes that flanked The Pleasure Walk, which led to the by then unused walled kitchen garden. Here in the summer term we would fill seven-pound biscuit tins with the tiny wild strawberries that grew there in profusion and take them back to the dorm for feasting upon. In early spring, the woods behind the house were carpeted with snowdrops. We would pick fistfuls of these and pack them in damp cotton wool inside tins, which we'd post home to our mothers. I wonder if they survived the journeys? In the autumn we'd go for long walks in the surrounding woods to gather chestnuts for roasting.

My special partners-in-crime were Jane Neave and Jill Nott-Bower – who were both, like me, rather precocious. We were fascinated to discover that some of the senior girls would take walks way out into the park beneath Heaven's Gate, where there was a hutted camp set up as a convalescent hospital for American soldiers. Rumour had it that they were all recovering from venereal disease! It did not take us long to suss out that these girls had assignations, and we enjoyed great sport stalking them and playing Peeping Tom. We'd writhe giggling in the undergrowth as we spied on these rather innocent courtships. We filled a little red notebook with strip cartoons illustrating what we'd seen. Mostly these depicted girls with enormous jutting breasts and Betty Grable hairdos teetering provocatively on ridiculously high-heeled shoes. Approaching them would be soldiers wearing Yankee-style forage caps (easy to draw). We'd draw dotted lines from the eyes of the soldiers to the nipples of the girls and from the eyes of the girls to the trouser-flies of the men. We thought this was wildly naughty and excruciatingly funny.

49

As in every girls' school at that time it was fashionable to have a 'pash' on a senior girl. Mine was called Sheila Gurdon. I think she was a general's daughter. There was a certain amount of snobbishness at The Royal School about one's father's rank. Sheila paid me no attention whatsoever. Nevertheless, I adored her.

It was a tradition of the senior girls during the long evenings of the summer term, when revising for their exams, to amble round and round the 'circle' that in those days linked the three main drives to the house – one from Warminster, one from Horningsham and one from Frome. On one such summer evening I was in the Ten Dorm gazing out and enjoying the view when the adored Sheila came into sight walking round the circle with her head deep into a book. Wanting to attract her attention, and hoping to solicit a wave, I took a garment (which by pure chance happened to be a pair of navy blue knickers) from a pile of newly returned laundry on the window cill beside me and waved it wildly at my pash.

It was Lord Bath's habit occasionally to entertain to dinner the commanding officer of the convalescent hospital, and this happened to be one of those evenings. At the precise moment of the knicker-waving, a jeep clattered over the cattle grid on the Warminster drive and turned towards the house. I quickly pulled back from the open window and in so doing caught the knickers on the latch and dropped them. They fell several feet before lodging jauntily on a stone parapet. The Ten Dorm being above the Great Hall, there was no first floor beneath the dormitory giving access to a window at that level, so I had to try with a tennis racquet to reach down and retrieve the offending underwear. This proved impossible. What could I do? The only thing was to pretend I'd dropped the knickers by mistake and ask the handyman to produce a long ladder and rescue them. Hutch, as always, jumping to the worst possible conclusion, immediately accused me of waving the knickers at the American colonel!

Soon after I went to Longleat, Daddy was posted abroad again, this time to North Africa, so once more we lost our Larkhill quarter. Mummy was lucky to find Pear Tree Cottage, a small thatched house in Pitton, a few miles to the east of Salisbury. To help with the outgoings we took in lodgers – Joan (a colonel's wife) and her daughter Anne. Pear Tree Cottage was L-shaped, with a small dovecote. Whenever I think of Pitton I can hear the 'coo, coo, coo' of those fluttery white birds. My mother and Joan each had their own sitting rooms and shared the kitchen. Upstairs we occupied two bedrooms and Anne and her mother shared the 'best bedroom', which was glamorously furnished in pale grey-blue satin, with carpet, curtains and bed-coverings all carefully matched. In the greenhouse we kept rather fecund mice and we also had black and white rabbits, a pair called Bubble and Squeak.

Anne and I were both potential delinquents. Anne had already been expelled from the Royal School (I cannot remember what her particular crime had been), and both of us delighted in being naughty. Again, as in Fleet days, my sister Carol bore the brunt of the mischief. She was always so *good*, which used to infuriate us. One day we all went riding on our ponies in Clarendon Woods – ancient woods planted to landscape what had been the royal hunting lodge of Clarendon Castle, of which by then only the overgrown foundations remained. Through the woods ran wide grassy rides – it was very picturesque. Reaching the middle of the woods, Anne and I decided we'd had enough of Carol, so we made her dismount, tied her to a tree, and then went home for tea, taking her pony with us. A huge joke. Of course, our mothers were furious and we were sent straight back to rescue the howling Carol and then to bed for the rest of the day with only bread and water for supper.

Holidays at Pitton were fun. There was plenty to do – ponies to ride, Batters (our dogs' home dog), Sox the tabby cat, rabbits and mice – and Carol to tease, as well as village children with whom to play hopscotch in the lane opposite the cottage. Sometimes we'd go in to Salisbury on the bus – on market day this was great fun as ducks and chickens would be transported in crates on the roof and everyone chattered all the way to Salisbury and all the way back.

Joan had a lover, which intrigued us. My mother disliked him intensely. He was a real smoothie and we called him The Drip.

Eventually my mother had enough, particularly as the Colonel was a friend and she felt guilty about condoning his cuckolding. Mummy had also discovered that her gin was disappearing at an alarming rate. Setting a trap by marking the bottle, she had to conclude that the missing gin was smoothing the gullets of The Drip and Joan. All this had tested the friendship to the limits and Joan was asked to leave. I was rather sorry to see her go – and even sorrier to say goodbye to Anne, my partner-in-crime.

There came a term at Longleat when I had behaved particularly badly and was given the punishment of not being allowed to go home for the holidays until a week after everyone else. This was not such a bad punishment as it was meant to be, because one of my friends – Jane Lane – also had to stay behind, because her parents were abroad and she had nowhere to go for the holidays. We had plenty of fun together and I cannot remember that we were supervised in any way. We found our way up onto the roof and danced around the towers – even standing on the parapets pretending to be statues. We crept about rooms all over the house, particularly enthralled by the State Apartments. We'd loll on the sofas of the Prefects' Room (the gallery overlooking the Great Hall), pretending we were prefects. We went wherever we liked. We found secret staircases and passages leading from spooky parts of the cellars – but they had rotten duckboards and we were too frightened to explore them completely. We made friends with Lord Bath's manservant in 'the Boot Room', where all the polishing of his shoes was done. And of course there was Steven to take for walks. We'd wander down to the Home Farm and spend hours in the woods, paddling in streams and picking wild flowers. It was all a little unreal.

By the end of the summer of 1944 I should have been leaving the junior Newland House and joining one of the senior ones – Marlborough (green), Havelock (pale blue), Wellington (red), Clive (purple) or Lawrence (yellow). Marlborough was my preference. At the end of the term we all wanted to discover to which house we would be posted. Everyone was told except me. I asked Hutch why I had not been told my new house, but all she said was: 'You are

PLAIN JANE

THE MARQUESS OF BATH
JOB'S MILL,
WARMINSTER, Wilts.
BAl2 8BB

0985 212279

28th March, 1985

Mrs. Jane Donaldson,
Catmint Cottage,
Hinton St. George
Somerset.

Dear Mrs. Donaldson,

Thank you so much for your very amusing and charming letter
concerning your experiences as a school girl whilst you were
at Longleat House during the war.

I only had the opportunity of meeting your Headmistress when
I came back after the war and I must say I found her a very awe
inspiring lady and I am sure that she ruled your establishment
with a rod of iron.   Nevertheless she and my father got along
very well together.

I suppose this good lady did have some cause for complaint as a
pair of knickers (which may I be so bold to say, were dropped by
mistake on purpose) were displayed in front of the House when the
Commandant of the American Hospital was getting out of his car,
but to put you in the category of a harlot was, I think, a bit
too much and I suppose the expulsion from the school which you
experienced was not only based on this incident but was of a
cumulative nature.   However, believe me I am not trying to criticise
you because I am so glad you enjoyed your stay at Longleat and I can
assure you that it made the last few years of my Fathers some of the
most pleasurable years of his life.   He loved you all dearly.

His Great Dane's name was Steven and he is now buried in the Pets
Cemetery at Longleat and I am sure would appreciate a litle posy — *Bath,*
of flowers on his grave should you ever visit us again.   *with love!*

As you say Longleat has changed but regrettably we have to keep up
with the times in order to keep up the House so I hope you will
forgive the necessary commercialism which has taken place.

Yours sincerely,

Bath

P.S. *Not on to the inmates at Bath — the Hospital, but I guess even some
of the members of the staff suffered from the unmentionable!!*

53

not yet ready to go to a senior house. You must first of all learn to behave like a senior.'

That was it. Even Miss Harding, the headmistress, said nothing when I was subjected to my end of term interview to be read my school report.

Mummy met me off the school train at Paddington station. I told her of my misery at the prospect of yet another year with Hutch as my housemistress and said how much I was dreading it without my friends to support me.

'Don't worry', Mummy said, 'you're not going back. They won't have you back. They have asked us to take you away.'

No more Royal School. And a summer holiday in Devonshire to look forward to ... What the hell!

Chapter Six

Towards the end of the time I was at Longleat, Mummy gave up the Pitton cottage. Her parents were by then living in a flat on the sixth floor of Peter's Court, near Whiteley's in Bayswater, and they had heard that a one-room flat had fallen vacant on the first floor of the same block. Now that my sister had also started boarding, at Parsons Mead in Ashtead, Mummy felt free to offer herself for useful war work – and this flat seemed ideally situated. She could find a job and she could keep an eye on her elderly parents at the same time. She took the flat.

Holidays were a bit of a problem though – the flat was really much too small. It had only one room, with a double bed that could be folded up into a cupboard during the day, a tiny kitchen and a weeny bathroom. We did rather get on top of each other. Carol had to share Mummy's bed and I either had to sleep on the floor or upstairs with Buddhi and Buddha. As a result, Mummy usually took us away somewhere for the holidays – sometimes to rather strange places.

Once, at Christmas, we PG'd with a mean-minded family outside Bishops Stortford where we did not get enough to eat. It was a cold winter and the house was freezing cold. One summer we stayed with an eccentric family in an interesting and isolated house near Lewes, where they kept goats and we had to drink goats' milk. The goats were always gnawing through their tethers and eating things.

Once it was the washing off the line, another time it was all the sheet music from the piano stool. They were rascals, but they provided much diversion. The house was not far from the railway line at Barcombe and we used to do dreadful things like playing last-across when a train was coming or putting pennies on the line to be bent by the train. I can remember, too, staying at a moated manor house in Kent, at Five Elms, where they took in lodgers – that was at Christmas time too, and we had snow and it was lovely. Sometimes we'd go to Scotland, to the Auld grandparents, travelling on the overnight sleeper from Euston to Glasgow.

This summer of 1944 we were off to Bideford in Devon to stay with army friends, the Keenes. Pat and Peggy Keene had been old friends of my parents since India days and they'd also served together since returning to England. They had five children, ranging from Brian, who was about my age, through to Michael, who was only about a year old. Pat Keene's mother, Granny Keene, had a large house on the outskirts of Bideford, at the end of an unmade-up road known as Raleigh. The house was halfway up the side of a very steep hill, and many steps had to be climbed through a shrubby rockery to get to the front door. Level with the house, a large garden had been laid out, with a lawn big enough to play badminton, cricket and croquet.

Granny Keene was totally blind, but she was a lovely old character and very tolerant of the tribe of children that had invaded her house for the whole of the month of August. We left her in peace for most of the day, as we usually trekked two or three miles via fields and winding lanes to Westward Ho! to spend the day on the beach. The fields alongside the house were erupting with mushrooms. Early each morning we'd go out and fill baskets with them to eat for breakfast – any extra unrationed food was manna in those spartan days.

Petrol, of course, was virtually unobtainable, and our Standard Ten car (US 5990) had been 'laid-up' for the duration of the war. We'd come down from London by Great Western Railway, and although Peggy Keene did have a car she had very little petrol and had to conserve what she had – hence the long daily slog to the beach on foot. It was worth the effort. The beach was vast and sandy, with lots of rocks and pools where we could paddle and fish for prawns.

In the evenings we'd play cards and board games, or join Granny Keene in her sitting room and listen to books on records that she was sent weekly from a library for the blind. Some of us would knit socks for soldiers; some of us would just loll about. It was very peaceful and the war seemed worlds away.

One of our treats was a stay for a few days with Peggy's parents, the Pengellys, who had a farm called South Yeo in the country a few miles west of Bideford, towards Clovelly. The farmhouse was long, low and cream-washed, with cool flagstone floors and lovely pictures and antiques. Peggy's sister 'Kitten' and her children were spending the summer holidays there, so there was a large and noisy family houseful. Mealtimes were amazing. We'd never seen so much food. Masses of meat and vegetables and salads and fruit pies and puddings sloshed with thick yellowy cream made in South Yeo's own dairy.

One day we had an expedition to Clovelly. We children rode there on bicycles, the last part of the ride along the Hobby Drive, a private track winding through the woods along the cliff edge and very steep in places. Lunching outside the pub down by the harbour I bit into a delicious crab sandwich and was viciously stung by a wasp. My poor lip swelled up like a big fat slug, much to everyone else's cruel amusement. Most days we'd take the dogs and ride our bikes a mile or so to the nearest beach to South Yeo, down a steep sandy track for the last few hundred yards. There were miles of sand and not a stranger in sight.

It was a heavenly holiday, but throughout it my mother had been worrying about my future. Where was she to send me? I had been interviewed by several headmistresses – but none of them found me in the least appealing. They naturally did not want to take on a twelve-year-old girl who had just been expelled from The Royal School. In desperation she even took me to an 'educational psychiatrist' who made me do a lot of puzzles and fit shapes together and asked me questions about various pictures she showed me. I was rather nervous at first, but she made it all seem fun, and obviously I did well because in her report she said I had an IQ of 150 and had intellectual powers of a very high quality. She also said that I would always be rebellious and anti-authority and that my emotional development would be slow compared to my intellectual progress: ('Her advanced mental outlook is also likely to get her into trouble against authority unless her excellent reasoning power can be enlisted on the side of law and order'). How true her predictions turned out to be.

In the end, Granny Auld came to the rescue. As mentioned earlier, before her marriage to Gag-Gag, Winnie Burton had been on the staff of St Columba's School in Kilmacolm, next stop down the railway line from Bridge-of-Weir. Later on her daughter Lirlie and my own father had been pupils there. Granny knew most of the staff well and she managed to persuade St Columba's to enrol me as a day girl. What good fortune! I adored Granny and I looked forward to going to live with her at the start of the autumn term.

Chapter Seven

It was good to be back in Scotland, and Granny and Gag-Gag welcomed me with open arms and no recriminations. Because of the war, life at The Grange had changed somewhat. There were no longer any living-in maids – only Edie who came in daily to clean and help with the cooking. The drawing room was seldom used and my grandparents had converted the old servants' room-cum-day-nursery into a cosy sitting room. The hall had been re-arranged to provide an air-raid shelter! A heavy-legged table had been thickly draped with rugs, and beneath it were mattresses, blankets and pillows. We never heard an air-raid siren, but if we did we were supposed to crawl under this table and wait until the all-clear sounded. In fact, we did take refuge there once, on the only occasion when we thought we heard enemy aircraft overhead.

In London, where the siren used to scream almost every night and the sound of exploding bombs was quite familiar, it never occurred to us to take shelter. We were totally fatalistic, and I cannot remember ever feeling afraid of the bombing, even when I was in London – although once the V1s and 'doodlebugs' began, one did feel a prickle of fear hearing the motor cut out close by. V2s were more damaging, but not so frightening because their engines did not cut out before impact, so there was no dark and pregnant silence of suspense.

Even at Longleat we had seldom taken shelter in the cellars, although air-raid practise was regularly carried out. I do remember one particular occasion when we had a real alarm and actually heard the droning of German aircraft overhead. It must have been at about 10.30 p.m. when the alarm bells sounded. We all left our beds, each girl taking a blanket and pillow with her, as we had been told to do, and filing in quiet and disciplined fashion along the top floor corridor, down the stairs to the Musicians' Gallery and on to the large landing at the head of the double-winged staircase which normally we were forbidden to use. Down the shallow blue-carpeted stairs we trooped, through the door leading to the cellar steps and thence to our appointed rallying posts to be counted.

Lord Bath had been hosting a dinner party that evening, and we gazed with admiration at his assembled guests wearing dinner jackets and elegant evening gowns. I can remember one particularly lovely dress in midnight blue crêpe with a plunging back; this was worn, we were told, by Lady Nunburnholme, a Thynne relation.

I got to know my grandparents really well during the year I spent with them. Granny's main love was her garden, and I adored helping her select and arrange the flowers in vases for the house. Under the staircase, by the servants' entrance to the dining room, was her 'vase cupboard' – she had lots of lovely vases of every possible size and shape. Granny was full of good works too and was very involved with the Girl Guides, in which she held a very senior position. She would go off to meetings dressed in her smart navy blue uniform with silver buttons and a big blue hat, upswept at one side where her large silver Girl Guide badge was pinned.

By now there was only one car – Granny's small Austin saloon. My grandfather had generously donated his brand new Wolseley 16 to the government to help with the war effort. Dear Gag-Gag was one of the most generous men I have ever known. He liked his roast beef, his whisky and a good cigar. He smoked too many Turkish cigarettes, which stained his fingers orange. He always seemed to be chewing horrid-looking things called charcoal biscuits – for his indigestion I suppose.

After a week or two to settle in, the time came for me to start the autumn term at St Columba's, where I was given a great welcome by the staff and made to feel rather special. Several of the mistresses had taught my father and aunt, so they took a special interest in me. I found that in Latin, English and mathematics I was way ahead of my class – but in French, history and geography I was definitely behind. The teaching at that school was excellent, however, and I worked hard.

Each morning I would walk down the hill from The Grange to Bridge-of-Weir station to wait for the westbound train from Glasgow to Kilmacolm. On the opposite platform waited the Paisley Grammar School boys, including Alastair Mitchell. Alastair had red hair and freckles and he was manly and strong looking. He had no time for girls. But oh, how madly did I fall in love and unashamedly flirt with him? I was only twelve at that time, but I was physically advanced. I'd 'started' or 'got the curse' already (which earned me considerable kudos with the more slowly developing girls!) and I was mentally precocious in the extreme. I did not know the true facts of life yet – I had only gleaned a few garbled and rather confusing details from gossip with other equally ignorant girls. Instinctively we all guessed that kissing on the lips was part of it, and at the Junior Society parties on Saturday evenings in Ranfurly Church Hall I'd always suggest that we play Postman's Knock and similar games. Eventually I did manage to make Alastair give me a fumblingly innocent kiss and to walk me home after the party. I was over the moon with joy and ecstasy, already anticipating the next thrilling excitement.

It did not take Granny long to cotton on to what I was up to, and she soon began to keep a close eye on my comings and goings – all of which were really totally innocent.

A girl called Maureen Muirhead became one of my best friends. Her father owned the Bridge-of-Weir tannery and he was rather rich. Maureen lived in what seemed to me then an enormous house, approached by a winding drive through trees. Quite a large stream ran through the grounds, falling steeply through a series of water-falls and pools – one of which was large enough for us to play the Scottish game of curling when the water froze.

Maureen had her own little hut at the edge of the woods in her garden. Here we and our friends would brew up tinned tomato soup (stolen from our larders at home) on a methylated spirit stove and eat it with bread or dog biscuits (dog biscuits are delicious with tomato soup when you are really hungry and eat them by the light of stolen candles in a blacked-out secret hut in the woods). We'd finish off our meals with illicit bits of cheese or cake, also filched from parental larders. The hut was furnished with deck chairs, orange boxes and old blankets. Scraps of fabric hung on string provided curtains with which to conceal our goings-on from grown-ups and enemies.

My other friends' names I cannot remember. Yvonne? Cherry? We were a gang. In Cherry's house, I learned to dance the quickstep and foxtrot. She had marvellous records – 'In The Mood', 'American Patrol', 'Moonlight Serenade', 'Shine on Harvest Moon' . . .

Memories of Alastair still linger. Our gang would bicycle out to the derelict clubhouse of an abandoned golf course near the Locher Burn to meet the boys. This was just a wooden hut, but it was a long enough bike ride away to be too far for Granny to police. We'd swim in the burn, which was very cold – and I couldn't swim anyway, so I hated it, but Alastair was there and I was determined not to be a cissy. We played lots of tennis too, but Alastair did not like tennis. 'Tennis' soon became the excuse I'd make to Granny when I was really going to meet Alastair and smoke a fag with him. Smoking fags was really sophisticated. Especially as I (rotten thief) used to steal fistfuls of Gag-Gag's best Turkish ones, which were a lovely oval shape and considered awfully chic by the others.

Sometimes Granny would catch me out. Once, waiting for Alastair by the ruins of Ranfurly Castle, I saw Granny striding over the golf course towards me. What was I going to do? Alastair was due to arrive at any moment. I had to invent an unlikely tale about searching for a comb that I'd dropped on a previous walk. Granny, like a sort of crouching spider waiting for its prey, pretended to believe me and helped me to look for the comb – hoping, of course, that Alastair would turn up so she could catch him red-handed and give him a piece of her mind. Fortunately Alastair spotted Granny before she spotted him, and he turned and ran like a stag till he was well out of sight.

Other assignations took place at Paisley swimming baths. I hated swimming, but I would go with my friends all the same because it got me a long way from Granny's suspicious eyes. After swimming we'd all buy bags of chips and eat them on the train home, each 'couple' romantically eating out of the same chip bag.

In my grandparents' eyes, Alastair was 'common', but Alastair was extremely brainy too, and I'm sure he will have done well in whatever sphere he chose to make his career. I wonder ...

I managed to persuade Granny to let me have a dog (by then Laddie and Jill were no longer). A trip was made to Paisley Dogs' Home, where I chose Lex, a silky-haired black and white mongrel. I loved Lex very dearly and took him with me nearly everywhere. Walking over the fields one day, Lex and I were greeted by a small Welsh corgi bitch from the nearby farm. She was evidently on heat and very enamoured with Lex, as he was with her. Before I knew what was happening they were coupling frantically. I had never seen such a performance before and was entranced, amused and a little frightened by it. However, when the act was over and the pair seemed unable to separate I became alarmed, thinking something had gone terribly wrong and wondering what on earth to do. In vain I tried to pull the animals apart, tears by then streaming down my cheeks. What was I to do? In the end, nature took her course. Lex was able to withdraw from his sweetheart, and his sweetheart trotted contentedly back to her farm. I had been highly intrigued by this performance and 'dined-out' on it in the hut in the woods later on.

In May of that year, the war in Europe came to an end and VE Day was celebrated. I remember a huge bonfire in the field next to The Grange, and fireworks and lights shining out from everyone's windows. There was singing and dancing and balloons, and the celebrations went on long into the early hours of the following morning.

But this was a sad time at The Grange, for Gag-Gag was far from well. In the summer he went into a Glasgow nursing home for an operation – I think it was for his prostate. I was very naughty and refused to go with Granny to visit him. I simply said that I hated hospitals and I was not going to visit anyone in one. I never saw Gag-Gag again. For in July I went down South again. And very soon Gag-Gag was dead. It was my first experience of death close to home and I was shattered by it. I had never thought it possible that people of one's own could die. I suffered agonies of remorse for not having visited him in the nursing home, for having been so selfish and insensitive by insisting on listening to the American Forces Network on the wireless, when he hated crooners and Glenn Miller music, and for stealing so many of his cigarettes. I had not been kind to that dear, white-haired, honest, patient and good man. I simply had not appreciated until after he was dead how privileged I had been to have him for a grandfather and how lucky to have enjoyed that memorable year with him and Granny at The Grange.

Chapter Eight

That August we spent two weeks in a rather gloomy guesthouse just off the seafront at Hove. Rita and Cynthia Palmer were with us – and so, too, was a boy with the unbelievable name of Bruno Charles Benedict Joseph Tustain. Bruno was meant to be paying serious attention to the study of the violin, and he was frequently made to stay behind in his room to practise whilst the rest of us went down to the beach. Sometimes Cynthia and I would stay behind too. Then Bruno would put away his violin and get out his ukulele and we'd have a sing-song instead. Bruno's mother weighed at least twenty stone, but she was completely unselfconscious and would don a vast bathing suit and prance about in the waves with the rest of us, or lie sunbathing alongside her spindly husband. An elephant would have looked spindly beside Mrs Tustain.

VJ Day was celebrated while we were in Hove. It was a sweltering hot evening and every window in the street was open. Opposite our guesthouse was a building where hundreds of sailors were billeted. They held a wild party that night with drinking, singing, dancing, fireworks and a huge bonfire in the street. Cynthia, Carol and I were forbidden to go down and join them, but we watched and waved from our upstairs window, fascinated by the goings-on below. The sailors cat-called and shouted to us to come down and join them – 'Hello Darlings!', 'Hello Lovelies! Come on down and have some fun!'. It was all quite bewildering. Japan seemed such a long way away and we children knew precious little about that distant war.

When we returned to London there was much shopping to be done at Gorringes, to buy uniform for my new school. At last Mummy had managed to find one that would take me – Charters Towers at Bexhill-on-Sea. The uniform was brown and gold. Flared gym-tunics with scooped necks (much nicer than the horrid dark blue square-necked things worn at The Royal School), with gold and brown checked blouses; brown blazer; brown Harris Tweed overcoats and brown felt hats with an orange and brown striped silk band.

Charters Towers was no ordinary school. Charters Towers was Angela Brazil and St Trinian's rolled into one – at least it was during the years that I was there. During the war the school had been evacuated to Milland House, near Liphook, and the autumn term of 1945 when I arrived was its first one back in Bexhill. The school was housed in four Edwardian red-brick houses on the north side of the old Hastings Road, linked at the rear by a long corridor to which various higgledy-piggledy extensions had been added. House One was the junior house, and one graduated through the houses to House Four, which had dormitories for the senior girls. The kitchens, dining room and 'wreck' (recreation room) were all in House Three.

Behind House Two, where most of the form rooms were situated, was a fairly substantial single-storey wooden extension housing the gym, one large and two small form rooms and, at the rear, the domestic-science kitchen. All the cloakrooms where we kept our gym shoes and hockey sticks were at the back of House Two as well, as was (most dreaded holy of holies) the Head's Study.

The school had been founded and was operated by a Mr and Mrs Finch (Arthur and Catherine), a middle-aged couple with two grown-up daughters, Hilda and Barbara (Allee). Barbara's boyfriend (she must either have been divorced or widowed, as there was no Mr Allee around), Ken Cullen, was a Brylcreamed ex-RAF PT instructor. After his de-mob he used to give all us girls training in athletics, and many of us were passionate about him. We were also passionate about the resident handyman, who stoked the boilers and fired the lusts of us pubescent girls. They were the only men with whom we had contact – apart from Arthur Finch (who was much too old) and Percy Denchfield, organist and choirmaster at St Peter's, the church in Bexhill Old Town attended by the school.

The rest of the mistresses were a motley and rather aged crew. Staff must have been hard to find in those days, because most females of the right age were either still in the armed services or working in hospitals or factories. The most memorable of those in charge of our education were The Trio – three inseparable and quite incongruous friends.

The senior member of The Trio, and much the strongest character, was 'Porky the Pig' (Miss Porter) who taught us art. She was a tall, striking woman, with curly black (dyed?) hair and spectacles. She actually wore a little make-up, which was different, and we approved. We gave her the least trouble, perhaps because we enjoyed her subject more than those with which the other two were lumbered. Also, it was harder to play Porky up because she was quite good at keeping order.

Next was Miss Fletcher, 'Flexy the Frog', who tried to teach us maths, science and biology. Flexy (Flex for short) was dumpy, grey and greasy, with pebble-spectacled froggy eyes and protuberant teeth. She was a bit of a groveller, and always dressed in greeny-grey Viyella and tweed, emphasising her strangely frog-like appearance. We used to play Flex up like mad in biology lessons, especially when she blushingly tried to explain how rabbits mated. Questions thundered upon her, prolonging the lesson interminably. 'But, Miss Fletcher, *why* does the rabbit's penis get stiff when it's infused with blood?' 'Doesn't it have any blood in it the rest of the time, Miss Fletcher?' 'If it doesn't have blood in it, Miss Fletcher, why doesn't it get gangrene and fall off?' 'Why doesn't the lady rabbit run away, Miss Fletcher?' – and so on and so on. Miss Fletcher sometimes got red-faced and angry with us, understandably.

Last of The Trio was Miss Meyer, 'Maisy Mouse'. A timid little subservient and rodent-faced creature, no more than five feet tall, with frizzy mouse-coloured hair and tiny hands and feet. She was the submissive one of the three and obsequious to the other two. Maisy suffered most of all from our pranks. Her subject was history, and she 'ummed-and-erred' her way from 1066 to 1485 in slow chalk-twiddling stages, brushing back her frizzy wisps of hair with a chalky paw and filming it with white dust. Somehow she managed to make this potentially enthralling subject as dry as crusts. To enliven her classes we would utter little squeaks and move around with tiny mouse-like steps, our teeth sticking out and our lips pulled back. Once, we set up an ingenious arrangement whereby we suspended a piece of cheese on a long cotton thread, draped over a convenient beam in the form room, just above the staff desk. I was in control of the thread, and at a suitable moment I gently lowered the cheese till it dangled temptingly in front of Maisy's nose. When she tried to snatch at it, quick-as-a-flash I pulled the string and whisked it out of her reach. Uncontrolled giggling ensued, which poor Maisy was totally unable to quell. Eventually the room quietened down, but not before I had been banished to the corridor for the rest of the history lesson.

English was taught by a delightful person called Miss Shelton. If she had a nickname it must have been an affectionate one, for we liked her – although I must confess we sometimes played her up, and she was hopeless at keeping order. She was a distinguished-looking white-haired lady, close to retirement age, and she had a pronounced limp. She retired at the end of the 1948 summer term to a pretty little cottage outside Hooe, a village not far from the school. During my last year at Charters Towers she would often invite a few of us out to lunch and tea at her cottage on Sundays. We'd all sit around in her garden, talking and eating sandwiches and cakes and sometimes doing odd jobs for her – bringing in wood, mending and painting her garden gate and mowing the lawn.

After two terms at Bexhill, having successfully settled the school back in its proper home, the Finches appointed a new headmistress, Miss Eileen McGarry BA FRGS, a thirty-eight-year-old go-ahead woman – tall, handsome and elegantly dressed, with piercing dark brown eyes and exquisitely manicured fingernails. She smelt delicious too – she liberally used Schiaparelli's 'Shocking'. Miss McGarry's ('Garry')'s arrival revitalised Charters Towers and began to instil some discipline and pride in our school into all of us. She quickly gained our respect and she enlivened our minds. With a degree in geography from Reading University and Fellowship of the Royal Geographical Society, she obviously knew her subject, and she knew how to put it across. Geography became the favourite lesson of many a girl from then on.

Once the reins had been taken over completely, the Finches decided to retire to London, to a very smart address near Harrods. In many ways we missed them, for they had given the place a 'family' atmosphere. But mostly we missed their car, for it was a really flashy American beast – a Hudson Terraplane. We were all into 'things American' in those days and admired everything that was extravagant and finished with lots of chrome.

My early misdemeanours at Charters Towers, apart from disruption of class, were quite mild – breaking ranks from the school crocodile outing into Bexhill to sneak into Fortes ice cream parlour for a quick knickerbocker glory; hiding in the changing cubicles at Hastings baths or Bexhill beach to read my book instead of joining in the dreaded swimming sessions; smoking shared Woodbines, and – of course – the occasional midnight feast.

I have already referred to St Peter's Church in Bexhill Old Town. About ten girls from the school sang in the church choir, under the direction of the aforementioned Percy Denchfield. A lovely man he was too, who managed to keep us quiet and orderly as well as to give us a love of church music and singing. Two of the main attractions of choir practice were male choristers Stanley Leppard, who had an evening job in a fish and chip shop, and his friend Bob, who worked in a bakery. Four of us girls got friendly with these two lads, both of whom were full of fun. One day they suggested, and we agreed, that it would be exciting to break bounds after lights-out and meet in a field for a midnight feast. They would bring fish and chips, buns and cakes and we'd have a good time. These excursions became almost weekly events. At about 10 p.m., when all was quiet in the school and no-one was about, the four of us would foregather and creep out of a back door and cross the playing fields to our assignation at the very convenient remains of a half-demolished haystack. We'd scoff fish and chips and buns, pass round a couple of Woodbines and generally enjoy ourselves before creeping back to our respective dorms.

Sadly, all good things come to an end, and inevitably we had to get caught. One moonlit evening we were happily enjoying our feast when we noticed the beam of a torchlight approaching from the direction of the tennis courts. *Cripes*, we thought, this is *it*. Hastily packing up fish and chip wrappings and extinguishing fags, we burrowed into the hay and tried to hide ourselves – but to no avail, for we had already been spotted. And it was Maisy Mouse, of all people, who had spotted us. The least likely one to be brave and go out alone at night with a torch. 'I know you're there!' she said, 'so you might as well come out!'.

Back to face Matron Maxted we were marched, and all hell was let loose. Next morning we were summoned to Miss McGarry's room to be sentenced. One of the worst punishments was being completely 'gated' for a whole month, unable to meet or even see the boys – and by now Stan had become 'my boyfriend'. It was a disaster.

Worse was to come. Stan was furious at being unable to see me and he decided to protest. Having attached an old pair of corsets and a dead rat to the end of a rope which he had tied onto the back of his bicycle, Stan rode up and down the Hastings Road outside the school yelling, 'Oi want Jyne, Oi want Jyne'. 'You've got to stop him,' said Garry. 'He'll ruin the school's reputation.' Out into the road I went, imploring him to stop – 'or else I'll *never* be able to see you again,' I told him. It did the trick. He said he was very sorry and took himself off, trailing the corset and dead rat behind him . . .

Stan was actually rather a respectable boy. He was studying the oboe at school and he later went to the Royal College of Music. He wrote to me from there once or twice and sent me Christmas cards for a couple of years, trying to convince me that playing the oboe was not cissy; nor was it cissy (he said) to be a male ballet dancer. 'You have to be really strong to be a male ballet dancer,' he said. I still felt that both activities were really a bit cissy. I often hear nowadays of important concerts being conducted by someone called Leppard – not 'Stan' Leppard, but I wonder if it could be the Stan using a more appropriate first name? I often wonder . . .

Hockey – I was the *greatest* at that. I was very fast. I played right wing and I could outrun everyone in the school except Marian Williams, who was a real sprinter and aspired to running in the Olympics. In the school sports I was always second to Marian in the 100 yards, but I could usually defeat her over the hurdles!

I have omitted to describe the woman who probably exercised the most control over all of us – Matron Maxted, a formidable female with an instinct for catching miscreants red-handed. 'Be sure your sins will find you out, Jane Auld,' she would say on the frequent occasions when she did catch me sinning. 'Maxted', as we called her, always wore a starched white coat and a triangular nurse's coif. She was thick set and heavy-featured, with flat feet and sticky-out teeth (why did so many schoolmistresses have sticky-out teeth in those days?), and she suffered severely from migraines.

Boarding school life in the immediate post-war era was not the comfortable existence it seems to be now. Although the form rooms had central heating of a sort, they were so draughty that one was never warm except when hugging a radiator. The dormitories, however, had no heating whatsoever – and we were not allowed to have hot-water bottles. I got round this stupid regulation by finding an empty gin bottle in Garry's dustbin. This I used to fill with hot tap water and take to bed with me. I can remember sharing a small two-bedded room at the top of House Four with Marian Williams, which was so cold that the water in our bedside glasses would frequently freeze solid during the night. It was too cold to get out of bed to dress; one simply stayed under the bedclothes and pulled on one's undergarments in the fuggy warmth.

House Four reminds me of 'Mamzelle', whose room on the first floor was immediately below the garret I shared with Marian. Mamzelle was truly and exotically French. Although past her prime by then, she was chic, with a heavily made-up face and smartly coiffed and dyed gingery-blonde hair. Mamzelle smoked incessantly, and although her wrists jangled with bright gold bracelets and her nails were always painted scarlet, her fingers were heavily nicotine-stained – and my, did she *cough* first thing in the morning! Mamzelle could not understand English girls at all and was shocked by our lack of modesty – because we'd run from dorm to dorm clad only in bra and pants, and we'd even undress and have baths in front of each other – no modesty at all! I would love to have found out more about Mamzelle. I always had the feeling that she must have a 'past' – and indeed I discovered, years later, that she had served with great valour in the Resistance and had been awarded a *Croix de Guerre*.

I was ever a bad influence on those about me, both at work and at play. Towards the end of my first term our form were all given timed intelligence-test papers to do. I found this test incredibly easy, as I had covered all the work during the earlier part of the term. This was probably because of the excellent Scottish education I'd enjoyed at St Columba's, Kilmacolm the previous year. Anyway, the following term I was moved up into a higher class, where most of the girls were a year older than I. Still I found the work easy, so I did not need to apply myself very hard. I messed about in all the lessons. Usually I managed to scrape through end-of-term exams by concerted swatting for a week beforehand. This was most unfair on my slower peers – but that fact did not, of course, occur to me until many years later.

Again, my school reports testify for themselves:

'Jane's conduct leaves much to be desired ...'

'She is still too noisy and uncontrolled for the senior form ...'

'Jane has the brains and ability to do much better. She must keep her mind on her work ...'

'... frivolity and inattention ...'

'Untidy. Does not set a good example. I expect a far higher standard from her in view of the time spent on her ...'

'Jane is a problem which so far we have not succeeded in solving, despite all our combined efforts ... '

'She is too much swayed by emotion, and her frivolous outlook on life prevents her from being a good influence.'

Eventually I did settle down, became a prefect and conformed (relatively speaking). My sins at any rate became more sophisticated – like having an account with William Hill. Being a prefect meant *privileges*, which had to be good.

The Prefects' Room led off the passage connecting Houses Two and Three. It was quite small, but in the corner it had a little fireplace where we could enjoy a coal fire and make toast. We also had a kettle that we could boil up for tea and milky drinks and concoct primitive snacks. The favourites were 'Corned Dog' (Pom instant potato mixed up with mashed corned beef) and 'Corned Cat' (Pom mashed up with sardines). Both were absolutely delicious eaten by the light of candles and a flickering fire. Other favourites were (inevitably) baked beans on toast and tomato soup. Yum, yum, yum – what memories of gastronomic delights return as I remember and salivate. We would sit for hours on end round that fire, discussing Life, Love and our Ambitions For The Future.

It was around this time of prefect privilege that I managed to acquire a cat. The first of many to enrich my life. The school caretaker's family cat had kittens, most of whom easily found homes. One of them, however, had the misfortune (no doubt because he

73

was being over-inquisitive, as cats always are) to cause an iron to fall off the ironing board and land on his nose, slightly deforming it (his nose, not the iron!). His nose was very, very pink. It was going to be difficult to find him a home, so I suggested to Garry that we might be allowed to have him as a prefects' cat. Permission was granted.

The kitten's resemblance to E.M. Shepherd's Piglet was striking, so 'Piglet' he became. Piglet was highly intelligent and a very quick learner. He was amazingly easy to house-train. His home was the Prefects' Room – which was quite a long way from any door to the garden. To save us having to take a long walk to let Piglet ('Piggy') out, we taught him to sit on a tennis racquet and be lowered onto the ground outside the window of the Prefects' Room. He would then trot off to do what was necessary, then he'd return to sit beneath the window and meow until we lowered the tennis racquet down to him, whereupon he'd climb back onto it and we'd carefully lift him back inside again. Not many cats are as clever as that!

Piggy soon became 'my' cat rather than prefect property. He took to sleeping on my bed and I took over full responsibility for feeding him. It was natural, therefore, that when the end of term came he should return home with me for the holidays. My mother was persuaded to accept this arrangement, and an open-fronted cat basket was found to accommodate Piggy for the train journey home.

Garry loved Piglet and became quite envious and broody. Soon she acquired a lovely tortoiseshell kitten of her own called Pente – because he arrived at Pentecost. The two cats became friends and made a handsome pair – Piglet's white and grey tabby fur being an excellent foil for Pente's gingery black.

Garry had a great friend, a Miss Dore – Headmistress of King's Lynn High School – who would sometimes come to Bexhill for weekends. It so happened that on one of these weekends, the school was to perform an entertainment for the staff. Each house was to put on an act of its own. As captain of my house, Sussex, I had the witty wheeze of writing a highly satirical skit lampooning the members of staff. It was extremely funny, but perhaps it was ahead of its time, and Garry was definitely *not* amused. In fact, she and Miss Dore got to their feet in the middle of the performance and left the hall in fury. I had gone too far again!

Indeed I had. Garry was really angry. I was suspended from being a prefect and house captain – a public humiliation. Fortunately, it was not long until the end of term, and at the beginning of the following one, Garry relented and I was reinstated.

Too fast those four years went by. It was such *fun* at Charters Towers and I really loved it there. Eventually, the last morning of my final term arrived. Up early to pack our overnight cases and get ready to catch the coach to the station after a quickly snatched breakfast. But Piglet was nowhere to be found. I was distraught. I refused to go home without him. There were tantrums and I would not get on the coach. Garry came to the rescue by promising to find him, put him in his basket and deliver him as soon as possible to Bexhill station to be conveyed, in charge of the guard, by the next possible train to Victoria.

Daddy had by then been posted to the Royal Artillery Depot at Woolwich, and we were living in a four-storey Georgian quarter at 57 The Common. That very same afternoon a telegram arrived from Bexhill: 'PIGLET ARRIVES VICTORIA 3.45 P.M.' Oh, the relief! Off we sped to collect him – he was none the worse for his journey in the guard's van, and extremely pleased to see us.

I kept in touch with Garry over the years, and after I retired I started attending the annual Charters Towers old girls' reunions, held at first in the house she shared with her friend Miss Dore in the picture-postcard village of Tarrant Monkton, near Blandford Forum in Dorset. I once made a special visit to her and took her out for a country drive with a sandwich and coffee picnic in a spot with a winning view. She was, by now, in her nineties and still as meticulously groomed and manicured as ever, with a memory and wit as sharp as ever, too. She wrote me a thank-you letter afterwards, from which I quote:

My dear Jane,
I find it quite difficult to express adequately my gratitude for the splendid day you gave me – from the arrangement and thought of it all you brought the lunch and then those photographs which renewed my memories of early Charters Towers so well and we were able to talk about each one and discuss your Report! How well you overcame your attitude in early days to become successful in your career and life and grow into the woman you are.

We celebrated her 100th birthday in 2009 in the pub at Tarrant Monkton. It was a gathering too huge to be held at Tarrant House. She was as lively and handsome as ever and full of party spirit. Miss Dore had died a few years before, which was sad, but Garry was well cared for by, and enjoyed the companionship of various dutiful Country Cousins. Then, in the early part of 2011, her health began to fail, and in May of that year, aged 102, she died.

I have always maintained that Granny Auld and Garry were the two women who influenced my life more strongly than any others.

Chapter Nine

Although the war had ended in August 1945, we had to stay on in the London flat for about a year because Daddy was still serving with the army of occupation in Austria, where he was thoroughly enjoying himself. He was stationed near the mediæval town of Bruck am der Mur, which was surrounded by mountains and forests. He had copied Monty's example and provided himself with a fully-equipped caravan, which could be attached to the convoy of lorries and guns whenever the regiment moved from place to place. He also managed to get hold of a rather grand ex-German Army staff car – a powerful Mercedes Benz with leather-strapped bonnet and huge spare wheels mounted on each side. It was a menacing looking animal and he was very proud of it. He enjoyed superb skiing, and was entertained lavishly by the local gentry, who offered him as much shooting and stalking as he could find time for. I still have three mounted chamois heads and several large chamois leathers, trophies from his time in Austria. In addition to all these blessings, he was allocated a young and beautiful Austrian countess as his interpreter, who accompanied him whenever he required her services.

Some of Daddy's earlier wartime experiences had not been quite so pleasant. When he had finished instructing at Larkhill he was sent to join the First Army in North Africa, where he was seriously wounded and had the lower half of the right-hand side of his face shot away. He wrote his mother a touching letter describing the details of his wounding:

Dear Mother,
This is American Red Cross notepaper, but it's a BRITISH hospital!
You'll have heard by this time that I've "copped one". Nothing serious, though extremely annoying as it impedes my eating, drinking and smoking. Also I shall have false teeth! (Not all, only the right side, upper.) It was our first real battle, and I had just got up to another of our Ops to get some information, but I found that the officer had been killed and so took his place till a relief should arrive (or so I thought). I'd just done one shoot when a shell splinter went through my right cheek and mouth, removed all the top row of teeth, knocked my pipe away and knocked me a bit silly.
When I came to, the two chaps in the OP were discussing my fate and tidying me up, and calling for stretcher bearers. I was bleeding "all over 'is clothes". I was able to arrange things better and also to point out that stretcher bearers would be a bit obvious up there, and anyway my legs were OK. I found my pipe! And stepped over the back of the hill where two infantry stretcher bearers tidied me up and I got my Sgt to wireless back to the Bty what had happened. I then started to walk back to the MO. I got a lift after a bit, and got back to the Doc, where my face was tidied a bit, and am now on my way "through the usual channels" to a beauty doctor who'll build me a new cheek!

Presumably he was well enough to return to battle, for he wrote to his father on the 23rd May 1943, describing some of his battle experiences after his wounding:

I took over the regt on 18th April, back from rest, and straight away moved up to recce areas near Midjez el Bab ready for the battle. We moved up our recce parties and were bivouacked on the night of the 20th in a little valley. During the evening a lot of shooting started about a couple of miles away. It got a bit closer but we thought it was just "patrol activity" and I continued to sleep. About three in the morning my Adjt woke me to say that there seemed to be a battle pretty close, and there was. Up on the road about 400 yards from our little valley. We got packed up very quietly and stole away to a more healthy place. Fortunately I had happened to have a look at a track leading away from our valley, away from the road, the day before and was able to take the party out in the dark.

Next day we discovered that the Bosche had intended to stage a breakthrough to our L of C, to muck up our preparation for the battle he knew was coming. He got a rude surprise and left a lot of tanks and vehicles behind on our gun area, which we moved into next night "according to plan". My taffies repaired one very nice armoured "half track" which I now use as a "forward command post".

Well, we moved in by night, and collected a nice lot of ammo, and supported the infantry battle to seize the "Important Strategic Heights" North East of Midjez.

These had to be taken before we could move our guns forward, as they overlooked the places we wanted to put them. I was delighted to hear that the one on our left, which had been a worry to us in January, was taken by the "Jocks" led by their Pipers (said Jocks coming from our locality).

On our own front the Bosche was determined not to give up the hills, and counter attacked again and again with tanks.

We, the regt, did a hell of a lot towards breaking up these tank attacks with our big shells; we were knocking them out with indirect fire. We were *definitely* credited with fifteen as *ours* must have helped with lots more.

Anyway, they never succeeded in interrupting our preparations for the final drive.

For that my lads started shooting at 4 p.m. on May 4th, and shot all night, at enemy batteries and counter attacks, then at 4 a.m. supported the infantry attack which was to punch the hole, and then at 8 a.m. both batteries moved off to support the armoured division in their breakthrough. From then on they were at it solid, working as horse artillery (only better than the RHA).

On the 7th the whole regt came under the famous armoured div which turned south and cut the main Bosche force off, and I had the whole regt to use, working with them. This was a real "cavalry" battle and I was with my battery commander up with the CRA having a front row view. I was a bit frightened at times, as mine was the only "soft" vehicle; they all had tanks in the armoured div and even my BCs had Bren Carriers. I had a wireless truck. When we broke through the Hammam position (said to be impossible by a Bosche general) as soon as the tanks had got through the village (after our guns had dealt with the anti-tank guns) and while the infantry were going in to mop up, the brig. pushed on to the far side. I had to go too and had visions of Bosches taking pot shots out of upstairs windows. However I was only attacked by a French frippet who leapt on to the running board and embraced me (she couldn't to that to a tank, so a "soft" vehicle has its points). We'd pasted the place so well that the Bosches were only thinking of surrender.

Next day we crashed on, halfway across the neck of the peninsula and rounding up Wop L of C troops in hordes.

We had a slight delay while we dealt with another lot of Bosches who were holding up a different div of ours. We shot our big guns up their arses and they decided to go. Then we punched right across the peninsula, leaving infantry to mop it up, and got ourselves in a position to paste the behinds of the Bosche and Wop Army that were fighting the French and 8th Armies. Our guns and the RAF hit them so hard and the tanks rounded them up and the whole outfit put up white flags. The Bosche, when he's not winning, is a miserable creature; he can't take a pasting.

I must say it delighted me when we ended the battle with one battery of mine ahead of the leading battery RHA and my *rear* battery was in front of most of them.

After the battle was over we had a lovely four days by the sea, working half days cleaning up and collecting "Booty" in the form of lorries, Rangefinders and all sorts of stuff, and the other half in letting the chaps rest and bathe. They needed it as they'd been going all out from 21st April to 12th May and were dead tired.

We've now returned to Tunis, and had our guns lining the streets for the Victory March. A grand sight. Led by the French troops, whom the lads cheered like anything (they'd fought with them in the south and knew lots of them). Then a party of Americans and then the British contingent, looking superb. They were led (after the generals of course), by my old regt. At the head of the marching column was my old battery, now commanded by Jack Carey, with their guns and vehicles polished as if for the Aldershot Tattoo.

He returned to hospital for many months, enduring several operations to rebuild his jaw and repair his face, but in spite of these operations he remained badly scarred for the rest of his life. He later served in Crete and Italy and fought his way through Greece and Yugoslavia before finally reaching Austria.

Back in England, Daddy's first posting was to Dundonald Camp in Ayrshire, which was close to two of the Auld ancestral homes, Dankeith and Underwood. After that he was sent to Westbourne Camp, near Portsmouth, and we moved into a large colonial-style bungalow quarter, one of three set within a large garden and surrounded by a twelve-foot-high yellowy brick wall. The bungalow, 11 Burnaby Road, was close to the naval dockyard and the railway line between Portsmouth Town and Harbour stations. This isolated little compound had miraculously not been damaged by the bombs that had devastated nearly all the nearby buildings – we sat on an island in a wasteland completely flattened by bombing.

Life slowly began to return to peacetime normality, although there was still rationing of food, sweets and clothing, and motoring was severely restricted by lack of petrol. It was difficult, too, to have to start to get to know my father all over again, having been separated from him for more than five years – which is a long time when you are a child.

Into our lives, soon after moving in to Burnaby Road, came 'Church', Daddy's driver and live-in batman. Arthur Church was a fresh-faced lad from the small Warwickshire village of Dorridge, near Knowle. He was a real mother's boy and highly domesticated. The rigours of national service life and barrack-room accommodation were not to his liking at all. He had chosen to become a driver, and for several months he had been chauffeuring my father's staff car. He was a smart fellow, with a good sense of humour, and he was excellent at his job and got on well with Daddy – and he was delighted to be allowed to become his batman, especially when he was told that he would be able to live in our quarter and have a room all to himself.

Church quickly became one of the family, just like a brother to my sister and myself. The silver was always polished bright, and he was keen to learn from Mummy the right way to lay a table and how to serve drinks and hand round the food at dinner parties. He loved cocktail parties. In his starched white jacket and immaculate khaki trousers he would perform like an experienced butler, and he had the knack of being friendly to the guests without being at all 'familiar'. He loved being part of the family, and we all became fond of him. He learned to cook quite well too – there was little to which he could not turn his hand. Shopping. Dog-walking. Ironing. Gardening. Feeding the dogs and cats. Washing the car. Nothing was outside his orbit.

I went to my first grown-up dance from Portsmouth, at RAF Thorney Island. Mummy insisted that I should wear a white dress. I was livid. I wanted to wear black. But in those days a girl's first evening dress *had* to be white – and in those days daughters did what their parents told them to do! So I wore a white dress. It was actually a lovely dress, in stiff white taffeta, with a halter neck and a full sweeping skirt. Stitched to the waistline was a single long-stemmed, red-silk carnation. I thought the dance was awful, except that I met up again with Anne Pasley, my fellow miscreant from The Royal School. By then she was married and properly behaved. I remember being horrified when I went to the lavatory because there were women being sick. Mummy and Daddy told me afterwards that you expected that sort of behaviour from the RAF!

I must have been about sixteen when the novel *Forever Amber* was published. It was considered to be an outrageously explicit book and I was forbidden to read it (I was not allowed to read the *News of the World* either!). I was never one to be put off when I wanted to do something badly enough – and I wanted very badly to read *Forever Amber*. Once the household was safely in bed at night, I would creep along to the drawing room, take the book from its shelf and tiptoe back to my room where, by the light of my torch, I would read until my eyes were sore.

At Portsmouth we acquired a Welsh corgi bitch, Chetchi (pronounced 'Chetty'). She was black and tan and very well bred, from the Rozavel kennels from which the Royal Family obtained their corgis. When she was old enough she was mated to a champion, Rozavel Thumbs Up, and she produced five fine puppies. Three we sold, but we kept a dog and a bitch – Monty and Baban. We also added two cats to the family – Fifi, silvery grey with oriental blood, and ginger and white Mr Peabody.

Our leisure activities were limited by the persisting shortage of petrol, but we spent summer holidays on the beach at Hayling Island (getting there by ferry from Portsmouth), sailing in the regimental yacht and picnicking in the Hampshire countryside. There was little for a teenage girl to do and I was glad when Daddy was posted to London, where he was given command of a regiment at the Royal Artillery headquarters at Woolwich.

We moved in to a large quarter, 57 The Common. It was a tall, early-Victorian house overlooking the common and a tram stop. There were six bedrooms, and a dining room large enough for our table to be fully extended to seat twelve in comfort. A simultaneous posting for Church allowed him to come with us, and he was given two small rooms on the second floor at the top of the house.

When I left Charters Towers I was seventeen and I had a whole year to fill in before I could start my radiography training at Westminster Hospital. Much against my will, but with great common sense, my parents insisted that I should take a secretarial course, and I was duly enrolled at 'Miss Toad's', a ten-minute walk from the house.

Miss Toad's was an extraordinary, Dickensian establishment. Miss Toad was enormous – she must have weighed over twenty stone. She always wore the same voluminous and completely shapeless, dirty-looking black garment. She smelt indescribable, like a dirty linen basket full of heavily soiled socks and knickers. She was a firm disciplinarian, and the other girls, most of whom were only about fifteen and from the humblest of homes and with very little education or confidence, were quite terrified of her. From the first day we were made to type in time with a metronome, with a felt flap over our hands obliterating the keyboard, so we had to learn to type by touch. It was a good way to learn, and I learnt quickly. Miss Toad was a born teacher, particularly if one showed aptitude and interest. Shorthand fascinated me, so Miss Toad put a lot of effort into helping me with it. She made it all seem so logical that it was with glee that I walked home at 4 p.m. each day to tackle my homework. It was no chore to me – I loved doing it.

Mummy encouraged me to play badminton in the evenings. I didn't like it much, but she said I would 'meet people' – meaning men. The only two I did meet were each, in their different ways, thoroughly unsuitable. One was a married major, who was at least twenty years older than I and whose wife refused to leave her native Devonshire to accompany him on his military postings. Because he was married, my mother assumed he would be a 'safe' escort for me. Safe he was not. He would walk me home after badminton across the dimly-lit common, and before long I had experienced

my first passionate kiss. After that, the walks home became inter-
ludes of sheer delight and titillation. He was even allowed to take
me to the theatre in London, and to military parties that Mummy
and Daddy were unable to attend. We'd return by the late train
from Charing Cross with a compartment all to ourselves, and many
were the romantic journeys we shared.

The second 'unsuitable' was a pink-faced nineteen-year-old called
David. His father was a captain who had come up through the
ranks (as had the major). His mother was a self-opinionated bossy-
boots. David was in the Merchant Navy and he knew no girls, so
when he came home on leave and we met he became a bit infatuated. He was painfully shy and never plucked up the courage to
touch me. While he was away on his tanker in the Persian Gulf
and such places he would write me long letters and send me nylon
stockings – but there were too many words and not enough action
for me, and by now I liked older men.

Then there was Donald McCullouch. My father's sailing friend.
He was a bachelor and lived in the War Office Mess in the former
Royal Military Academy buildings at Woolwich, a hundred yards or
so up the road from our house. He spent most of his evenings
with us, helping Daddy in his workshop in the cellar or yarning
with him in the drawing room over a pipe and a glass of whisky.
I fancied Donald, but he treated me like a child. He was a most
elegant man and he dressed beautifully. When I began commuting
to Westminster Hospital for my radiography training he was working
at a desk in Whitehall and we would sometimes travel on the same
train up to Charing Cross. I felt proud to be seen with Donald in
his city-gent suit, gunner tie, bowler hat and rolled umbrella.

Wonderful military balls were held in the Mess at Woolwich. The
men all wore their 'blues' and looked quite splendid, their tight,
tight trousers with stripes down the sides making their legs look
like those of racehorses. The regimental silver would be displayed
in the supper rooms and there were tasselled programmes with little
pencils attached in which dances were 'booked'. You had to stick
to the programme; it was insulting to miss a dance when you had

been booked. My programmes were never very full and I was always a bit of a wallflower. I imagine this was partly because I still had a disfiguring scar on my forehead. Partly, too, I scared men off a bit because I wore a lot of make-up and pretended I was very sophisticated and clever. Also, I never met anyone in an informal way. The dinner parties that my mother gave before the balls always consisted of my parents' middle-aged friends, with one terrified young subaltern dragooned into being my partner for the evening – enough to scare away even the most worldly young man. Having been 'detailed' as my escort, they naturally itched to get away from our stuffy party to join their own wild subaltern friends and their debby partners. Nevertheless, I revelled in these balls. The music, the unlimited champagne, the flowers and the tasty breakfasts of bacon, eggs, sausages and tomatoes served before 'carriages' at three or four in the morning.

Once I went to a naval ball in the Painted Hall at Greenwich Palace. I attended a presentation garden party at Buckingham Palace, went to rugger matches at Twickenham, saw nearly every play and musical in London and enjoyed one or two debutante dances. I had a good time. Princess Margaret came one day to receive the Freedom of Woolwich. We were given VIP seats outside the Town Hall, quite close to the Princess (who was my heroine at the time), to watch the military parade, led by Daddy mounted on a charger! He hadn't ridden for years, so a lot of practice had been put in beforehand.

The short train journey to the West End meant that Church spent much of his time off enjoying the bright lights, and he began to lose his provincial shyness. On one occasion, as he was dashing out of the house to catch the train to London, he saw my season ticket lying on the hall table and thought he'd borrow it to save the fare. Unfortunately, when he showed it to the ticket collector at the barrier the man noticed the large 'W' (for woman) printed across it, took a second look at Church and charged him with travelling on a borrowed season ticket. He had to go to court and was fined for this offence.

Church made several friends in Woolwich, one of whom was called John Fox. He was the manager of a gentlemen's outfitter in the town. Gradually it dawned on us that this friendship with Fox was becoming an emotional attachment. Shock. Horror. One evening there was a lovers' tiff, and Church, who had retired to his rooms at the top of the house, refused to come downstairs and talk to Fox, who had obviously called to try to make up their quarrel. Church shouted and screamed abuse down at Fox from his window, finally proceeding to fling out all the gramophone records and other gifts that Fox had previously given him.

One weekend I had an old school friend to stay. Jackie Cameron-Smith had gone on from Charters Towers to finishing school at Les Avants in Switzerland. Jackie was a smart girl and she lived in a flat off Pont Street. Her father had a furniture factory in the East End, where Jackie worked, and she used to travel to work on the underground with her Siamese cat on a lead! When she dismounted from the tram at the stop outside our house, she was most elegantly dressed in a white silk dress with a white pagoda-shaped straw hat and long white gloves. Church spotted her walking towards the house and came rushing through to us in the kitchen: 'Mrs Auld, Mrs Auld, come quickly – it's Miss Jackie, and she's done up all Chinese!'.

In February 1952, King George VI died and Princess Elizabeth became Queen of England. We went to pay our respects at the lying-in-state in Westminster Hall. The queue stretched two to three people deep from the Houses of Parliament back towards Millbank, across the river and turned back again to pass alongside St Thomas's Hospital. It took four hours to reach the head of the queue, which continued to grow all the time. My feelings were overwhelming as I entered the dimly-lit, silent hall and saw the late-King's coffin, draped with the Union flag and watched over by four guardsmen in full dress with their heads bowed over their reversed rifles. That ancient and echoing hall was something never to be forgotten, nor were the expressions on the faces of every mourner who paused by the coffin to pay his respects to this much-loved monarch.

We were privileged to be allotted seats in a room overlooking the Tilt Yard of the Horse Guards' building to witness the Royal Procession following the King's coffin from Westminster Abbey. I saw HRH The Duke of Windsor for the first time, following on foot behind his brother's cortege in company with the Dukes of Edinburgh, Gloucester, Kent and other royal princes. Behind them came the carriages bearing the heavily veiled royal ladies, including the new Queen Elizabeth II. It was an historic occasion, and I was very proud to have witnessed it.

That summer I took and passed my exams and became a fully-fledged radiographer. It was convenient timing, as Daddy was leaving Woolwich and was to be posted as O/C Troops on the *Empire Windrush*. During the year we had spent many weekends visiting the Essex/Suffolk borders to look for a house to which my parents could retire. We eventually decided upon The Old Mill House at Wix, near Manningtree, and we all looked forward to moving out of London and into the countryside again.

Chapter Ten

So, now that I was qualified as a Member of the Society of Radiographers I had to look for a job. As the family was settled in The Old Mill House at Wix, in Essex, I approached the Essex County Hospital in Colchester. Unfortunately they had no vacancies, but they did offer me a post at Black Notley Hospital, near Braintree. This was a former TB sanatorium, now an orthopaedic unit. The hospital was out in the sticks, so the job was a residential one, living in a cottage in the grounds. I got plenty of work experience, but social life was non-existent and the other radiographers were really not very exciting. Mercifully, after only a few months, a post did become vacant in Colchester, so I was able to live at home and travel into town daily by bus.

This job was in complete contrast to Black Notley. There were about six radiographers, including a male student, Norman, a great character. We all worked hard, but we had plenty of laughs as well. In charge of the department was a former nursing sister – Sister Akam, or 'Akey' as we called her. She was a mousy little creature, but she was always beautifully turned out, with a dark-blue dress, starched apron, cuffs and frilly lace cap. She had quite a job to discipline our little bunch of girls – and Norman. I was the only radiographer to have been trained at a London hospital, which earned me a certain amount of kudos, but we were a very good team and we all worked extremely hard.

I became friendly with one girl in particular – Heather Waite. Her mother was the Matron of a 'loony-bin' called Turner Village, and Heather lived at home with her. The other girls all lived in the nurses' home. The time came when Heather and I found living with our parents somewhat restrictive, and, after much discussion, we decided to find a flat that we could share. We found one at 43 Lexden Road, which suited us perfectly. The flat was in what had once been the chauffeur's quarters and it was above a large garage. Our landlord was a gracious old man called Mr Pawsey, who had a housekeeper called Joan. Both of them were very kind to us. Each of us had difficult times persuading our parents that we wanted to leave home, but eventually they became used to the idea.

By then, Heather was being courted by the Consultant Radiologist, Rees Rhys-Lewis, 'George', (a Welshman, would you believe!). He lived in a small cottage in West Lodge Road at that time, which was conveniently close to 43 Lexden Road. Heather and I began then to have quite a good social life. We patronised the Garrison Officers' Club, where there were tennis and squash courts and social events. Mummy and Daddy also used the club, and one day I was sitting with them, watching the tennis, when I spied a devastatingly handsome man playing rather a good, elegant game. I wondered who he was.

One early evening, a couple of weeks later, Heather and I were having a game of squash when I became aware that we had an audience in the viewing gallery behind us. I became quite self-conscious, and soon we packed in our game and went to the bar for a drink. We were followed. Heather, who had lived in Colchester since leaving school and who knew a lot of the 'people who mattered' in Colchester, introduced me to these men who had been watching our rabbity game of squash. One of them was one 'Sir B', he of the tennis game. It was a portentous introduction. He was to become the dominant person in my life for seven years (and more) thereafter.

Sir B had a small advertising agency in Colchester. He also had a rather beautiful wife, two children and a handsome house in a nearby village to Colchester. Nevertheless, he set about courting me and I was completely swept off my feet. Sir B was a Robert Taylor look-alike – only he was even more handsome than the actor. He dressed elegantly, in well-cut tweed suits and Norfolk jackets. I had always been interested in advertisements, particularly those in American magazines, so his work interested me. As did his knowledge of history and classical music, encouraging me to read biographies of many historical characters. He really opened my mind to things that had never previously been awakened in me.

Soon we were having picnic lunches out at Abberton Reservoir and other romantic locations, and then early-evening assignations either out at country pubs or in our cosy little flat at number 43 or with George and Heather at Merly House. George Rhys-Lewis had, by then, moved across the road from his West Lodge Road cottage to a large Victorian five-bedroomed house.

As I got to know Sir B better, he obviously felt he could take a very brave step and offer me some startling advice. Ever since I had been ill when I was four years old, I had had to live with a disfiguring scar on my forehead. It was not just an old skin wound, for I had lost quite a few pieces of bone out of my forehead, so there was quite a deep ravine on my face. I had learned to live with this, and indeed I really was almost unaware of it. However, Sir B said I should see a plastic surgeon and have something done about it. He said it would change my life, because he said that it must put people off me, especially men. I took his advice.

The consultant plastic surgeon who held a clinic once a month at the Essex County was one Dickie Battle, from St Thomas's Hospital in London. I knew him in a professional capacity because he used to ask for me to take the X-rays of his patients. So I got an appointment and soon I was down at Hydestile Hospital, a satellite of St Thomas's. I had the operation, which consisted of scrapings being taken from a pelvic bone and inserted into the front of my face. For three weeks I stayed in hospital, and my hip was extremely painful for most of that time. For a further three weeks I had two very black eyes. Dickie Battle was a musician, into traditional jazz, as was George Rhys-Lewis – indeed they had both in the past played in the band at the Embassy Club in Bond Street. Many were the parties at Merly House, listening to, and dancing to, Sid Phillips and other bands, with George playing along with them on his clarinet.

Once my black eyes had gone and the swelling had subsided, I was amazed to see my new face. It was an incredible work of art that Dickie Battle had done for me, and there's no doubt that it did change me. I became a lot more confident and was always pleased when people congratulated me on the change in my appearance. And dear, dear Sir B; I was to be ever grateful to him for giving me such wonderful advice.

Among our many acquaintances at that time was one John Hollington. John was a bachelor in his thirties. He was full of fun and he had a vintage 4½ litre Bentley and a Healey. He was like a brother to Heather and me, and he would often squire me to dances at the club to make up parties with George, Heather and other friends, as I did not have an official boyfriend. At such dances, Sir B would always dance with me and pay me court and I fell more and more under his spell.

Next, I was to meet another man who was to become important in my life – John Main, who had a nice MG saloon car. John and Peter Main were brothers, whose parents lived in a beautiful Elizabethan house called Spout Farm, in Boxford, Suffolk. I cannot remember how we met these two, but Peter took to Heather and John took to me. We had a lot of fun together, sometimes spending nights at Spout Farm. The trouble was that John, too, was a married man, although he was in the process of getting a divorce. He was married to a Miss Siddeley, daughter of the owner of Armstrong Siddeley motorcars. This divorce meant that he had to beware of the 'Queen's Proctor', the vigilante to make sure people in divorce cases kept themselves squeaky-clean as far as their sex lives were concerned. John was in the jute industry, and to get away from temptation he undertook a three-year posting to Calcutta.

By then I had come to love John, in spite of my ongoing

infatuation with Sir B, so it was with real heartache that we said our farewells when he set off by ship to India.

Nevertheless, I continued to have fun and lots of parties. Heather and George grew closer, and so did Sir B and I – although I missed John terribly. At Merly House, George had room for his grand piano and some large pieces of good antique furniture. He also had a room big enough to act as his consulting room, so he was able to build up a healthy (well, not-so-healthy!) private practice. Knowing I could type, he asked if I would act as his secretary/receptionist every Thursday afternoon when his private patients consulted him. I was able to square this up with Akey, and so the arrangement was made, and it worked well.

During all this time our dear landlord, Mr Pawsey, was suffering gradually worsening health, and after a time he died. This meant we had to find somewhere else to live. By now each of us had a dog – mine was Tina, a corgi, and Heather's was a miniature poodle called Cliquot. Luck was with us, and a friend of Heather's told us about a cottage in Lexden called The Little Glebe. This was a single-storey, very picturesque building, with one huge reception room with a kitchen off it and one large bedroom with a bathroom off it. Heather was not too keen about having to share the bedroom, and nor was I, but we arranged the room in such a way that we each had plenty of space. Little Glebe was wonderful in the summer, but in the winter it was *freezing*. We used to have terrible difficulty getting the fire to light – we didn't seem to have heard of fire-lighters then – and so we were always cold.

The cottage was perfect, too, for my clandestine love affair, for it was at the end of a cul-de-sac off the Lexden Road and very hidden from prying eyes. Life with Sir B was all picnics, intimate lunches and occasional forays to his house to spend romantic nights there and lazy summer days in the garden when his wife was away from home. Inevitably, the worst happened and I got pregnant. The gynae consultant at the Essex County Hospital tried to be helpful by prescribing pills and castor oil and gin. I remember spending one New Year's Eve in a hot bath, swallowing a cocktail of these medicines – but of course they were to no avail. So began a desperate search for an abortionist – because, of course, abortion was still strictly illegal in those days.

Word went round the bush telegraph, and eventually I was given the name of a Polish lady gynaecologist and I got an appointment to visit her in her Harley Street consulting room. She arranged for me to attend a nursing home in Hendon and I duly arrived there one rainy February afternoon. Next morning I was wheeled into the operating theatre, which was immediately opposite my room, and strung up on the operating table. Rather disgustingly, I could see an enamel pail on the floor, with several aborted foetuses in it – very unpleasant, but I was so relieved to know that I should shortly be rid of this embarrassment inside me that I could happily ignore it.

When I awoke it was to the sound of weeping and wailing emanating from the landing outside my bedroom door, which was quite frightening. I rang for the nurse and asked her what was going on. 'Oh!' she said. 'There's a circumcision ceremony going on in the room next to you, and it is the women who are excluded from the ceremony; they are weeping and wailing – it's tradition.'

Money had to be found for this illegal operation – £100, no less, which was a large sum in those days. I found £50 by pawning my gold bracelet, and Sir B found £50 by selling his camera. When my father happened to visit the jeweller in Colchester to whom I'd sold my bracelet, the jeweller produced it, knowing Daddy was my father, and told him I'd obviously sold the bracelet because I was in some sort of trouble. Dear, dear Daddy bought the bracelet back, and a little time later handed it to me. He said he didn't want to know why I'd had to sell it, but said I was never to mention the incident to my mother; never, never.

My father had always been very protective towards me, which unfortunately resulted in a most embarrassing incident. Word had somehow reached my parents – via a friend of Mr Pawsey's housekeeper who happened to know my mother – that I was having an undesirable relationship with a married man. This person knew of him and revealed details of the whereabouts of his advertising agency. Goaded by my mother – for my father was not an aggressive man – he paid a visit to Sir B's offices and stormed into his room, accusing him of damaging the reputation of his daughter. He told Sir B that if he didn't put a stop to this philandering he would come back and give him a thorough horsewhipping! Fortunately, Daddy drew the line at actually carrying out this threat.

These events somewhat clouded over Sir B's and my relationship and he took fright. For some time, he avoided me and did not call at Little Glebe. It was a very unhappy time for me. I felt he was being very cruel by abandoning me at this very difficult time. However, in due course he regained his courage and we took over where we had left off.

At the same time as all this was happening, other social avenues were opening up. I had cousins on the Keelan side of the family called Pisani – John, Patrick and Elizabeth. Their father had died in the war and their mother had died of cancer a few years later. My parents virtually adopted Patrick, and he became more like a brother to me. He made his home in a caravan in our orchard at Wix, although he had by then joined up in the Royal Navy, so he was away quite a lot of the time. It so happened that his minesweeper and a couple of others were tied up for several months at Harwich, and through Patrick's connection, Heather and I were invited to lots of parties on board HMS *Bevington*, Patrick's ship, and others in the flotilla. The captain of Patrick's ship was one Rupert Craven, who had a veteran Rolls Royce and who took a fancy to me and squired me to dinners and the Saturday dinner-dances at the George Hotel in Colchester. He also treated me to drives in his veteran Rolls Royce – his pride and joy.

The parties on board the ships were fairly wild. As they got wilder, young midshipman Patrick used to be dismissed to his cabin. I remember one rather frightening occasion when Andrew Arnott, captain of one of the other ships, was returning home when he missed his footing and fell between *Bevington* and his own ship. Man overboard! Ropes had to be thrown down to him and he had to be hauled back on board, soaking wet, amid much hilarity on everyone else's part!

Heather and I were well treated by our admirers. We were squired to parties and theatres in London, often catching the 3 a.m. milk train back from Liverpool Street to Colchester – and having to be back on duty at the hospital by 9 a.m. in the morning. Among the shows I remember attending are Marlene Dietrich at the Café de Paris, and on another occasion Eartha Kitt (that time I was taken by the aforementioned Andrew Arnott).

Of course we were always broke – spending all our money on clothes, cosmetics and scent. Often we'd have to walk to work because we could not afford the bus fare. Also, we could hardly afford to eat, except when we were taken out to meals by our boyfriends. We made a cunning plan. The junior doctors 'lived-in' at the hospital and were provided with early suppers. We used to go along after they had finished and beg any leftovers 'for feeding to our dogs'. Actually, the food was for ourselves!

Life has to move on. John Main was expected back from India at any moment and I was agonising about my feelings pending our reunion. It so happened that a telegram suddenly arrived telling me he was arriving in Colchester the very next day – which, coincidentally, was the date of the Medical Ball at the club. George managed to get hold of two extra tickets and invited us to join his party for the evening. John arrived, looking heart-stoppingly handsome in his dinner jacket. I didn't know what to feel. It didn't help that I had several dances with Sir B, which made me feel dreadfully guilty and torn in half – especially when he said to me, 'Jane, you cannot marry that man – he is not for you.' Back at Little Glebe, John and I were finally alone. It was a difficult night. I did love John still – but somehow the success of Dickie Battle's surgery had changed me. I did not feel any more that I wanted to marry John, or anyone else, at that time. He had written me so many loving letters from Calcutta (which I still treasure), but I had to tell him the truth. He was wonderful, understanding, kind and affectionate. A couple of years later we did meet again and we had one cosy last dinner together in his London flat, near Archway underground station. He told me that he was about to marry an air hostess, a widow with a young son, and he was very, very happy. I was genuinely pleased for him.

The catalyst that brought about the next huge step in my life came about one winter evening. It was a Saturday and I was due to go home to Wix for the weekend. Heather and George were going to a party in Frinton that evening, so I asked him if they could give me a lift home to Wix on their way to Frinton. George seemed reluctant, but agreed. However, when we reached the crossroads in Wix he stopped the car and said, 'That's as far as I'm taking you – get out.' I was shocked and bewildered. I learned later from Heather that he thought my parents' house was close to the crossroads and they were late for the party already. Heather told me that George hadn't really wanted to go to the party and he was in a bad mood at the time! I had Tina on her lead and a suitcase to carry, and it was just about a quarter of a mile to Old Mill House. Luckily there was a handy phone box, so I rang Daddy and he came to pick me up.

I was extremely angry. Poor Heather naturally had to side with George, but at the time I blamed her for doing so. I decided it was time for a change. Heather and I could not live together in an atmosphere that was so horrible. I decided that I must make a complete break and seek my fortune in London. I had outgrown Colchester. I found myself some temporary digs in Maldon Road, with a nice old lady who was happy to have Tina as a lodger. I did a short brushing-up course on my shorthand and typing and then I felt I was sufficiently equipped to get myself a job up in the smoke. John Hollington, our dear 'brother', came up trumps. He was about to go off skiing with his girlfriend, and they offered me a temporary stay in her flat in Chelsea.

It had all been great fun for nearly five years. But things had to change. I felt I had to get free of Sir B – for he had always admitted to me, with supreme honesty, that although he loved me sincerely, our futures could not be together because he simply *had* to have a rich wife as he had such expensive tastes. . .

Chapter Eleven

And so I set off for London, with considerable trepidation, with only £12 in my purse and a hungry dog to feed. John's girlfriend's flat was in a basement just off the King's Road and it was fairly sordid and very damp. I only had a camp bed to sleep on, so Tina and I cuddled up together to keep warm. In one of her more generous gestures, Mummy had contacted an old family friend, Eve Dalby, who had a two-floor flat in Ashburn Place, off Gloucester Road. Eve said she'd be pleased to have me as a lodger at a reasonable rent, and so I moved in. It was a large flat, and the room she gave me had big French windows leading out into leafy communal gardens. It was ideal, because I could leave Tina in my room, with the windows open, while I went out job hunting.

Within three days I had succeeded in finding a job with The London Computer Group. Salary £7 a week! The offices were in a very old house overlooking Quaglino's, in Bury Street, off Jermyn Street in Mayfair – very handy for Fortnum & Mason! We were housed there by courtesy of the NRDC (the National Research and Development Council). Above our offices were those of some very high-powered computer programmers. It was the very early days of computers and the only users at that time were accountants, researchers and financial departments of companies such as The National Coal Board. Our two bosses were both accountants – Anthony J. Bray MA ACA and John Hough. Working with me was Daphne Aldis, who was to become, and remains, one of my very best friends. Daphne was a qualified librarian and she was auburn haired and strikingly beautiful. We were a great team and we worked extremely hard organising membership, meetings and the publishing of *The Computer Bulletin* – later to become *The Computer Journal* as membership grew and the group was promoted as The British Computer Society.

The Computer Journal was a great improvement on the *Bulletin* (which had been produced in the office on an ancient Gestetner machine, often with the pair of us toiling under the midnight oil into the small hours). The new *Journal* was much more up-market and was printed by Unwin Brothers of Woking (who also, at that time, were the printers of *Country Life* magazine – then still being produced by lovely old letterpress machines). However, it needed finance. With my long-standing interest in advertising, since school-days and more recently because of Sir B, I suggested to the bosses that I might be allowed to sell space to raise money. The Society agreed and paid for me to attend a course on advertising, allowing me time off for lectures one day a week. And so I began to contact all the manufacturers of computers and the associated suppliers to them. I was pretty successful, and this was appreciated.

In due course we moved to larger and more suitable premises in the City, in Coleman Street, not far from The Bank of England. This was not such fun. It was further to travel each day and there were no shops to indulge our lunch hours. I began to think: 'I'm busy selling space, which is not very exciting. Why don't I hop over the fence into the realm of creative advertising instead?'

And so it was that I applied for the job of assistant to an account executive at Notley Advertising in Hill Street, off Berkeley Square. My interview was with a Mrs Billinghurst – 'Billie' – who handled the account of Sanderson Wallpapers, Paints and Fabrics. That sounded just right for me, with my passion for interior design and decoration. I liked Billie immediately. She was not young, but she was very experienced and had a wonderful disposition. I felt that she liked me and I was optimistic for my chances of getting the job.

Filled with hope, terror and also with joy because my interview had been successful and the opportunity I had dreamed of was now a reality, I arrived for my first day at 15 Hill Street, the beautiful and historic house decorated by Robert Adam, with fantastic painted ceilings and a grand marble staircase. It was said that Nell Gwynne had once lived there. Now the house and the one next door were occupied by this small but extremely prestigious advertising agency, Notley's, founded by one Cecil D. Notley ('CD') just before the war.

Billie, my new boss, greeted me with a warm and smiling welcome and took me up to her third-floor office. Across the street was a yawning bombsite, rampant with pink rosebay willow herb, where two or three Georgian houses had been demolished by the Germans during the Blitz.

I loved the job, and I loved Billie. She went out of her way to teach me how to organise schedules and bookings and how to manage the creative people – and what a talented lot these were: Trevor Cox (William Trevor), Peter Porter, Ted Lucie-Smith, Peter Redgrove, Oliver Bernard, 'Sarzy' Sarzano and Assia Wevill. Those are some of the many names that come back to me after all these years. To make things even more perfect, I was able to take Tina to work with me and to give her lunchtime walks in Berkeley Square! A lot of wine was consumed as inspiration to the creative teams, and it was always fun to join in and to meet up at lunchtime or at the end of the day at the Coach & Horses, the local agency pub.

I was also given opportunities to work briefly on other of the agency's accounts, to get more experience – Clarks Shoes, Wolsey knitwear, Bourne & Hollingsworth, Swan Vesta matches. I was learning a lot. The firm also sponsored me to take time off to study for the exams of the Institute of Practitioners in Advertising, which I eventually took and passed.

By now I had moved on from Ashburn Place and was sharing a small first-floor flat with two other girls at 140 Warwick Way, behind Victoria Station and within view of the clock on the tower of the BOAC headquarters. Tina was a wonderful dog, and a great

101

companion, and she coped without complaint over my various moves. One of the girls was a designer for Marks & Spencer and she often brought home unused designs and fabrics for us to share. There were two other flats in the building. In one lived two young barristers, who went off each morning with their fabric 'barrister bags' over their shoulders and fraternised with us over coffees and glasses of wine. One of them had an MG sports car, and one Saturday morning he gave Tina and me a lift to shop in the King's Road. Tina and I were browsing in Peter Jones when she was suddenly caught short and peed on the carpet. I was mortified, but the staff were wonderful and made nothing of it – just mopped up the floor and said I wasn't to worry about it!

The other flat was occupied by two prostitutes, whom we rarely saw. During the night they would arrive home with clients in taxis, which they would ask to wait outside while they practised their trade. The slamming of doors and the ticking over of meters was somewhat disturbing, but we did get used to it.

Back into my life, then, crept dear Geoffrey Warland, whom I had known during my time at Colchester in Little Glebe – still a bachelor gay (in the old sense of that word). I had warmed to him by then, although we shared a strictly platonic relationship and he had several other girlfriends as well as myself. He took me out quite often, usually to interesting pubs and good restaurants. Once, with his friend Harry Hawker and a girlfriend, we went out to dinner at the Embassy Club and then on to the Four Hundred. I've still got a book of Four Hundred matches from our table there.

One memorable afternoon at Notley's a few of us decided to take a boat out on the Serpentine to get inspiration for producing a 'house ad' – an advertisement for the agency itself – scheduled to appear in the programme of some charity event. Trevor Cox brought along his portable typewriter and I took along an agency camera. Beautiful Assia Wevill, wearing an exotic straw hat, and a couple of other copywriters bearing bottles of Champagne came along as well. The party was captured on film and the picture used to illustrate the house ad, which was captioned: 'We really live our work at Notley's'. The photograph has since been used in one or two biographies of Ted Hughes, Sylvia Plath and Assia Wevill.

Assia's life was indeed a tragic one, which has since been sensitively documented. She was a friend of mine, but not a very close one, so I was not party to the events that were unfolding at the time and was only to learn the full details from the several books that have subsequently been published.

I was happy enough at Notley's until Billie, who was a widow, met and later married a Mr Pimlott and decided to give up her job and enjoy retirement. By then I was not experienced enough to replace her, and another woman, Pam Horner, was appointed. She had been working at Yardley in charge of all their printed matter – showcards, posters etc. She and I did not hit it off. I could not stomach being her underling, when by then I knew a lot more about actual press advertising than she did, so I decided I would have to move on. When I left, CD wrote me a charming letter of farewell, saying he was sorry he could not say goodbye to me personally but he was down in Street immersed in Clarks shoes. Visits to Clarks were definitely non-alcoholic and visitors were housed in temperance hotels. CD said he always took a well-stocked suitcase with him for his personal consumption!

The best way to climb up the salary scale was to move agencies, gradually moving up the pecking order. I went first (mainly to get away from Pam Horner) to Gollings, then Baker Dorset, on various not-so-exciting accounts. During this time I studied and passed the exams of the Institute of Practitioners in Advertising, which also helped my career prospects. At one point I applied for a job as account executive on the Terylene account. I was given a couple of interviews but heard nothing for some time and gave up hope of getting what would have been a very good job. Eventually the disappointing letter came, and I quote from it:

I am sincerely sorry to have to tell you that despite much cogitation we have reluctantly to conclude that there will be no opportunity on the Terylene account which would be suitable for your ability and status. It seems that whilst there is a very junior post to be filled there would be very scant possibility of both client and our own people *agreeing to a woman going forward into the full executive post.* Since this is the only role into which I can see you being satisfied . . .

Nowadays, no one would dare to admit to such a reason for turning a woman down!

However, good fortune was then to shine on me in the form of an approach by Notley's for me to return to their fold. Mary Scott, the account executive who handled the Bourne & Hollingsworth account, was about to retire and they would like me to replace her. Mary (a Canadian), in the late 1940s and early 1950s, had been a very successful copywriter and she had ended up with B&H and Caperns birdseed – a strange combination you might say, but she was eccentric. She had a budgie of her own, which always accompanied her in its cage to work. When I was working with Mary in the take-over period, I noticed she always had a glass of milk on her desk. She said to me: 'I'd better let you into my secret. There's a nice tot of whisky in that milk – it's what keeps me going! I always keep a bottle in the drawer.'

So I returned to find I'd been given a lovely big office of my own, in what had once been a bedroom and which had built-in cupboards with hanging space, a bar and a wash basin. It was luxury indeed. Tina still came to work with me every day, but she had to be banished up to the attics where the typographers were based. One in particular, Bob Large, became very fond of her and he would sometimes walk her for me at lunchtimes when I was busy with suppliers or clients – Christopher Bourne of B&H and his advertising manager, June Thompson. B&H published seasonal fashion catalogues, and part of my job was to oversee the finding of locations in which to set these, the briefing of photographers, the choosing of models and supervising the shoots. Often I also wrote the copy, especially for the Christmas catalogue – the contents of which were a bit boring for 'proper' copywriters!

Meanwhile, my career was hugely enjoyable and reasonably stable – if anything in advertising is ever stable. I had heard again from Sir B, who told me that he too had left Colchester and had managed to find a good job as a creative director at Colman Prentice & Varley (CPV), another very prestigious agency situated in Grosvenor Street. He wanted to see me again. The flame did not quite re-kindle, but we did occasionally meet up. He explained that his life was in trauma and his wife was divorcing him. He had a new girlfriend whom he hoped to marry. She was a copywriter at CPV and she was a general's daughter. She was also rich enough to support his need for the good things in life. In time he married her and they had a son together. Sadly, as he told me later, she eventually left him 'for a chap with a Debrett-featuring blood-line'. I still loved him dearly, and indeed I loved him till the day he died – and I still sometimes indulge in memories of those old Colchester days. He often took me out to dinner, and even stayed a few nights with me after I had left Warwick Way and was living in Joanna Bindley's 'annexe' in Lennox Gardens. We remained friends for the rest of his life – being in touch each Christmas by cards and telephone calls.

At most weekends I deserted London, either to go home to my parents at Wix, to Lirlie, my godmother's, or to my Great Aunt Jessican, both of whom lived in Gloucestershire. Lirlie and her husband Pat lived near Kemble on the main railway line to Gloucester and Wales. I used to catch the 5.45 p.m. express from Paddington, *The Cheltenham Flyer* (steam drawn, of course), which I think only stopped at Reading and perhaps Didcot before Kemble – so it really was a top-notch express. On one exciting occasion I was dismounting from the train at Kemble and struggling with Tina and my luggage, when the dog slipped her lead and fell onto the line. All the station staff rushed to my aid and they did manage to catch her and bring her back to me – but I held up this alpha-express for nearly five minutes!

I was earning a good salary by then and was able to indulge myself in nice clothes. In fact, I made nearly all my own clothes, but I could afford to use expensive fabrics and buy lovely shoes and handbags. My future looked very bright.

I much looked forward to my annual fortnight's holidays, which I always took in August in order to be able to spend them with my Aunt 'Uncle' Mary and her husband Lionel Carey in Scotland. The Carey family had a holiday house in Kincraig, 'Morven'. It was a large enough house to sleep about ten and it had a big garden, at the bottom of which ran the main railway line from King's Cross to Inverness. Tina and I would catch the 10 p.m. train from London and travel in a first-class sleeper in great comfort. Dogs were not allowed, officially, in the compartment – but the kindly attendants would usually turn a blind eye. I always slept well, and it was very exciting to wake up very early at Blair Atholl and be blinded by the beautiful Scottish scenery unfolding before one's eyes. The train stopped at Newtonmore, Kingussie and then Kincraig before continuing on to Inverness.

It was traditional in the Carey household that if a guest was expected to arrive at Kincraig station (which they were due to do at about 7.30 a.m.), the whole household and all the dogs would turn up on the platform in kilts, or draped in rugs masquerading as kilts, to give one a wonderful welcome. Then there would be a huge breakfast, followed by the making-up of packed lunches to take on our daily expeditions to favourite locations up Glen Feshie or the Lairig Ghru and climbing the mountains of the Cairngorms. Lionel and Mary Carey's two sons, William and John, loved to fish in the burns or the nearby loch on the River Spey, which ran along across the other side of the railway line. One day we decided to trek a long way up Glen Feshie and to stay a night in one of the bothys – we hardly slept at all on the rock-hard flagstones, but in the early dawn we woke to find deer close beside the bothy, munching the grass and drinking from the Feshie's waters.

In the evenings, after dinner, we'd all collect round the sitting room fire discussing the events of the day, drinking whisky and making plans for the next day's excursions, possibly to go shopping in Kingussie, the next village. The Carey family had bought

Morven in the early 1930s – and it is still owned by the third generation down, the Godfrey Carey family.

The return journey to London was most exhilarating, yet sad because I was leaving Morven for another year. The train left Kincraig at about 7.30 p.m. Once Tina was settled in my compartment, I would go down to the restaurant car to dine as the sun was getting low in the western sky and the mountains were glowing pinky-orange. To me, the scenery of that part of the journey was better than anywhere else in the world. That the train was hauled by steam made the journey even more romantic.

Going back to work was quite exciting too. I was in my element in the world of advertising and there was never a dull day. If it snowed or if there were strikes, Tina and I would happily walk to work through Kensington Gardens and Hyde Park to Mayfair.

Chapter Twelve

Coinciding with the continuing progress of my career, my social life was coming on nicely too. Having met Joanna Bindley on the train travelling up on a Sunday evening from Manningtree to Liverpool Street, I learned that she was looking for someone to share her flat in 42 Lennox Gardens, off Pont Street. Joanna was the niece of one of my mother's friends who lived in Bradfield, the next village to Wix. The flat had a separate little guest room (probably once a maid's room) off the second-floor landing. The bedroom/bed-sitting room had a wash-hand basin in an alcove and there was a separate lavatory. The windows overlooked the roofy landscape of Kensington museums and Brompton Oratory, with the trees of Kensington Gardens in the far distance. What more could I want? I had independence when I wanted it, and Jo's companionship when we were both at loose ends. I moved in during August 1957 – and my social life spiralled by several degrees. I transformed my little 'suite', furnishing it with a divan and chest of drawers, curtaining off the basin alcove and alcoves that had hanging space for clothes, shelving and room for a little Baby Belling cooker.

Jo was the perfect flatmate. She was the greatest fun, she was very sociable and generous – and she had many amusing friends. She was divorced from Mr Bindley, but she evidently had reasonable financial support from him, for she had lots of lovely clothes and each year was allowed to buy a suit from the couturier 'Michael'.

Through Jo, I made many new, fun friends and was introduced to lots of well-heeled gentlemen escorts who squired me to smart restaurants, nightclubs and race-meetings, and I began to live quite a hectic life, as well as doing well with my career, through which I also met an exciting range of people from writers to artists, fashion photographers and top models. It was a good time, then, to be in London.

By now I was earning enough to think about buying a flat for myself, and quite quickly I found the perfect choice – a second-floor flat with sitting room, bedroom, kitchen and bathroom at 5 Cornwall Gardens, off Gloucester Road in South Kensington. It was an elegant, late-Victorian house, and the rooms were a decent size; the ceilings were high, with handsome cornices, and the tall sash windows were of perfect proportions. There was also a small balcony overlooking Gloucester Road – useful in emergency when I could pop Tina on it to do her wee-wees! The ninety-nine-year lease cost £2,500. I moved in on the 12th June 1960. Independence at last. I was terribly excited!

It was at about this time that I saw a notice in the 'Births' column of *The Times* that Heather had given birth to a son, Jonathan, in St George's Hospital. I had often stopped to think nostalgically about Heather and that unfortunate event that somewhat spoiled our friendship. I thought the time was now right to try to forge a re-conciliation. I wrote her a letter congratulating them both on the birth of their first baby. Heather got in touch and we met up again and started back where we were before the drama at Wix cross-roads. From then on we met from time to time – but of course I was working and playing hard in London; Colchester was quite a long way away. Sadly, George died – he was, of course, a lot older than Heather – but not before he was able to enjoy his growing family of grandchildren. Heather was eighty in 2010 and she gave a fantastic party at a restaurant on the banks of the Stour, *Le Talbooth*, which I remember well from my Colchester days.

Betty Rendlesham was one of the first new friends I made through Jo's introduction. She had been divorced from Lord Rendlesham many years before we met and she had worked for some time in New York for Slenderella, a slimming and cosmetic company, and she was now working for them in London. She had a somewhat tempestuous relationship with her man, Paddy Barthropp – a distinguished Battle of Britain fighter pilot who had spent the last few years of the war as a German prisoner. On the day I first met Betty it was in the flat at 42 Lennox Gardens. She was visiting Joanna after attending a smart wedding, so she was dressed to kill and wearing a delicious flowery hat. She was also wearing very dark sunglasses, explaining that she had hit her head on a cupboard. Later, she told me that she'd actually had a fight with Paddy during which they both exchanged punches!

One of the couples to whom Joanna introduced me were Dick and Leily Austin. He was a musician and was head of the Opera School at the Royal School of Music. He had previously been conductor of the Bournemouth Symphony Orchestra. They lived in an attractive mews cottage off Sussex Gardens in Bayswater. They loved dogs, and were always happy to have Tina to stay if I was up to things where she would not be able to accompany me. It was through them that I met one of my most interesting men, Jack Gerber. Jack, too, was a musician. He played beautifully on his grand piano in his grand flat in Albion Gate, on Bayswater Road. He was South African and he was also extremely rich. He was a friend of John Huston, the film director, and one of the most exciting periods in my life centred on a short couple of weeks with Huston and his girlfriend, a French actress. Jack took us all to Ascot races one weekend and we then went to dine with Huston in his suite at Claridge's. Jack had once won a classic race at Ascot with his horse *Punchinello*, and the huge gold cup had pride of place in his apartment. After dining we four went nightclubbing – first to the Casanova, then to Churchill's and lastly the Cabaret Club. Another night it was the Milroy after dining at The Ivy. John was showing his girlfriend the top places to visit while she was in London. On the following Monday we all drove in Jack's Rolls Royce to have lunch and stay at Moyns, an ancient and very beautiful house near Newmarket belonging to Ivor Bryce, a rich racehorse trainer. Also in the party were Bobo Sigrist, an American within the Princess Margaret set, and her film-director boyfriend, Kevin McClory. The next weekend we were off to the July meeting at Newmarket and then back to dine at Albion Gate. We went racing at Sandown and did still more nightclubbing, at The Embassy and The 400 Club. It was a short, exhilarating and exhausting month before Jack went back home to South Africa. We never met again . . .

At the end of July I went with Daddy, Mummy and my sister to a Royal Artillery Ball at Shoeburyness. I thought it was pretty dull stuff until I noticed a group of handsome young men splashing about in a fountain. One was stripped to the waist and – wow, was he attractive! We were introduced and the electricity was immediate. His name was Robin Pink and he was a captain in the regiment. We danced that evening and he asked me to go to the theatre with him the following week. I cannot remember the play, but I do remember that we dined at Quaglino's – which was nostalgic for me as it was right opposite 29 Bury Street, my office when I first went to work in London. Robin took me out quite regularly, once to another ball at Shoeburyness and several times to the theatre, until he was posted to Germany. We did not actually keep in touch after that, but I later heard that he had been killed by one of his own regimental guns whilst on manoeuvres in Germany. I was very shocked to hear about it and I wished I had appreciated him rather more than I had done.

Another (in)auspicious introduction, for which either Jo or Leily and Dick were responsible, was to David. As usual for me, it seemed, he was a married man seeking extra companionship. David had been a pilot in Coastal Command during the war and later flew for BEA. He then set up one of the first 'sunshine holidays for the masses' travel agencies, which prospered mightily. He was fun and interesting and he entertained me very generously, even sending me a freebie on one of his firm's trips to Puerto Soller in Majorca, where I stayed alone because at the last minute he said he couldn't come with me. I suspect he had never intended to come, because he thought he might have got caught out! Never mind, I enjoyed the holiday in spite of that. He chose super places to dine – I remember only a few: Helene Cordet's Club, the River Club, Les Ambassadeurs. There were lunches, too, at Charlie's Bar, the 500 Club, Rules in Maiden Lane and others – I was taken to nearly every glamorous eating place London had to offer in those days. I was utterly spoilt.

Once I took over one of Joanna's cast-offs, an ex-guardsman who was, or had been, editor of either *Woman* or *Woman's Own* and had written a book *Fighting With The Guards*. His flat was next door to 42 Lennox Gardens and he was very charming, if a little *too* smooth – we referred to him, unkindly, as 'the head waiter'. He was an interesting and generous escort. We used to dine or lunch frequently at The Guards Club and he took me to the party to launch the musical *Expresso Bongo* and a couple of days later to the first night. Many years later I met one of the stars, Elizabeth Allen, affectionately known as Dizzy Allen, who had come to live in the next village to mine, and as I had been presented with the LP of the show I was able to play it and listen to her lovely gravelly singing voice again.

I cannot leave out another friendship from these memoirs; for some reason I christened him 'Penguin'. He was a consultant surgeon at one of London's greatest hospitals and he was very good company. Our favourite restaurant was Beoty's, a Greek bistro close to my flat near Kensington Close. Of course he was yet another married man, and unfortunately I knew his wife quite well. Once or twice I had driven her down to the Barthropp's fishing lodge, The Price of Peace, in Devon. On one occasion, driving back to London very early on a Monday morning, we saw dawn breaking to the east, behind Stonehenge.

I don't remember much about another of Leily and Dick's other introductions, to a German, Wolfe. I do have memories, though, of a fantastic trip with him to Paris. It was my first ever flight, by Alitalia, and that in itself was exciting. We stayed in the luxurious

Hotel Napoleon, close to the Arc de Triomphe, and we visited the Crazy Horse Saloon and the Folies Bergère. I nicked one of the hotel's coathangers, which I still use. On another occasion we went by train to Coventry where we were met by a chauffeur from Jaguar, as Wolfe was going to take delivery that day of a new XK120. We were given an interesting tour of the factory, followed by lunch in the directors' dining room, before driving back to London. Wolfe only visited London occasionally, as he worked as an interpreter for the WEU and his home was in Dusseldorf – where I presumed he had a nice German frau, girlfriend or wife. Men!! Just a day or so before I was due to leave for Paris I felt very feverish and was convinced that I was getting flu. Jo sent for her doctor, Peter Vernon, who came and administered an injection of I know not what. He told me that it would remain effective for two to three days, after which I'd feel pretty ill again. It worked just the way he described and I was very grateful to him.

Peter was my doctor from then on, and he became, and remains to this day, a great friend. It was another truly platonic friendship. He was the house doctor at the Dorchester Hotel, and he was called out on the famous occasion when Elizabeth Taylor was staying there and became very ill, necessitating a tracheotomy. Peter and his girlfriend Alicia spent many weekends with us a few years later when we had moved to Dorset.

Through Betty and Paddy Barthropp I was to meet many, many highly decorated wartime pilots. In particular the 'Killy' Kilmartins and Brian and Leslie Kingcombe, who were very close friends of the Barthropps. After leaving the Royal Air Force, Paddy and a fellow officer, Laurie Kelly, decided that they would each buy a new Rolls Royce with their 'golden bowlers' and set up a posh car hire business. They stripped off the insignia from their RAF uniforms and dressed themselves as chauffeurs. They soon built up a clientele of celebrities and well-heeled clients and the business prospered, so they were then able to employ chauffeurs instead of having to do all the driving themselves. Most famously, Richard Burton and Elizabeth Taylor were regular clients.

I spent several holidays with this coterie of the Barthropps' friends at The Price of Peace on the banks of the River Taw, near Hatherleigh in Devon. We did a lot of drinking and had a great deal of fun, especially at Christmas and New Year's Eve parties there – and these get-togethers continued for several years. Once I had met my soon-to-be husband, Arthur Donaldson, he would somehow manage to come too, which made everything even more romantic!

Chapter Thirteen

I first caught sight of Arthur Donaldson at the reception after the marriage of Betty Rendlesham's daughter, Caroline Thellusson, at the Hyde Park Hotel. I saw this tall, handsome, fair-haired man in a dove-grey morning coat, pink tie and smoking a cigarette in a long holder. My feet felt all funny and I thought, 'My God, what a handsome man!' I never got to meet him on that occasion – but I was not in any hurry at that time.

The second occasion was at a small drinks party in Laurie and Daphne Kelly's cottage in Glebe Place. I was chatting to a couple near the sitting room door when I spotted him again, standing by the window and using his cigarette holder to emphasise whatever point he was making. I turned to a woman beside me and asked her, 'Who is that man by the window?' Her reply (having misheard me) was: 'He's not fat – he's my husband!' She was Gwynneth, Arthur's second wife. I was told that she had previously been married to a baronet, Sir John Heygate, by whom she'd had two sons (John Heygate had previously been married to 'SheEvelyn', whom he had pinched from 'HeEvelyn' – Evelyn Waugh).

A few months later Betty Rendlesham rang to ask me out to dinner to make up a foursome with Paddy and a friend of his. When I told her I didn't want to meet any more married men, she said the friend was *happily* married but his wife was away at the time; he was being lent Paddy's cottage in Eaton Mews South and they felt they ought to entertain him. Betty knew that by then I was a bit off married men, but she assured me I would be quite safe with Arthur Donaldson. She succeeded in persuading me to join them.

We dined in a small restaurant not far from Chelsea Cloisters and had a happy and amusing evening, returning to the mews for coffee afterwards. Paddy and Betty then left, cunningly leaving Arthur and me alone together. I made moves to leave as well, but Arthur persuaded me to stay on, and later he reluctantly agreed to drive me home and leave me at my front door. That was the night of the 16th of April 1960. Arthur told me that this was a lucky day for him, because he had joined the Royal Air Force on the 16th of April and he got his first corgi, Morgan, on the 16th of April.

I learnt from Betty that Arthur Donaldson was the youngest of four brothers, all of whom were educated at Christ's Hospital, financed by the Freemasons because their father, a solicitor, who was a leading freemason in Seremban, Malaya, had died suddenly – leaving his wife, Gwen, a widow at the tender age of 28. Three of the brothers joined the Royal Air Force before the war. The eldest brother, Donald, emigrated to New Zealand under George V's scheme to become farmers. The second, John William, had been killed on active service, drowned when HMS *Glorious* was sunk off the Norwegian coast. Teddy, the next in line, won fame when he broke the World Air Speed Record in a Meteor in the 1950s. After he retired he became Air Correspondent of *The Daily Telegraph*. All three men won distinction and many medals between them – Arthur gained a DSO, two DFCs and an AFC. Their mother went thirteen times to Buckingham Palace to witness her sons being decorated for gallantry.

It was many years before I learned the full story of Arthur's service life, for – like most brave men – he was always reluctant to talk about his exploits.

Listening to his older brothers talking about their flying experiences when they were home on leave, Arthur was entranced. Having been apprenticed to Metropolitan-Vickers in Manchester after leaving school, he obtained permission from the company to release him temporarily to join the RAF. He learnt to fly and passed out as an 'exceptional' pilot. By September 1939, when war was declared, he was an instructor at the Central Flying School at Upavon on Salisbury Plain. By coincidence, a few miles away at Larkhill lived a seven-year-old girl who, nearly thirty years later, would become his third wife! Arthur wanted to be there with the others, fighting, but the powers-that-be insisted that his rôle as an instructor was vital and would not release him. Eventually they gave in, but he always felt that he'd missed out by not taking part in the Battle of Britain.

He was soon to command 263 Squadron, flying Westland twin-engined Whirlwind fighter/bombers and was based first at Yeovil and later at Exeter. On one occasion someone neglected to switch on the warning light indicating that the balloon barrage was up over Yeovil. As he approached the airfield he found himself surrounded by balloons and steel cables – but he managed to slalom through and landed safely.

It was whilst flying a Whirlwind that he achieved one of his most spectacular escapes. He was leading a sortie to attack the German-held airfield at Morlaix, in Brittany. Just as the squadron had released all its bombs and was turning for home, Arthur was hit by anti-aircraft fire. He completely lost consciousness, and when he came round he found himself skimming the waves. His Perspex canopy was shattered, his helmet was riddled with bullet holes and he was covered in blood from skin wounds to his head and limbs. His head was aching violently, but he managed to concentrate sufficiently to get the aircraft back across the channel and land it at Exeter. Ambulances and a stretcher party were waiting, as one of his fellow pilots had shadowed him home and radioed ahead of the emergency. As he was being loaded into the ambulance he asked where he was being taken to and was told, 'The Imperial Hotel, Torquay'. Unfortunately it was then not a five-star hotel but a military hospital.

His next excitement was Malta, where he distinguished himself in the fighting of the last decisive battles with the Luftwaffe in this area. Here he lost two fingers during a dog-fight, but he managed to get back to Takali airfield and to land, in spite of the tarmac being ablaze with many incendiary fires. For this exploit, he was awarded an immediate DSO. While he was being invalided home in the bomb bay of a Lancaster, the pilot came in to refuel at Gibraltar but overshot the runway and landed the aircraft in the sea, where it broke its back. Only Arthur and four other passengers survived – one of them being the famous Canadian fighter ace, 'Screwball' Beurling. Arthur was lucky to be able to scramble out through the hole where the back of the aircraft had broken, but he suffered further injuries in the accident – mainly burns to his arms – and he was temporarily hospitalised in Gibraltar to await his journey home. During his stay in hospital he was visited by the Governor of the island, who asked if there was anything he could do for him. Quick as a flash, Arthur replied: 'Yes sir; get me home in a destroyer!'.

The day after the Barthropps had organised that momentous meeting with him, Arthur phoned and asked me out to dinner. I accepted. And so it all began and blossomed. However, not long after our meeting the worst happened and I got pregnant, in spite of using that horrible contraption the Dutch cap. So it was back to Harley Street and a return to the Hendon Nursing Home. Arthur used to say that he only had to fly over a girlfriend's house in his Spitfire to get her pregnant!

Arthur was working at the time with Paddy at Belgravia Car Hire, and part of his job was to collect and deliver cars to various parts of the country, so we had exciting trips to Yorkshire, Scotland – all over the country. Once, driving down the A1 on our way back from a night at Peebles Hydro, we stopped for a picnic in a field somewhere in Yorkshire. A lovely sunny day and a tasty picnic with a bottle of wine – and I left my handbag behind in the field. By the time I realised it was missing we'd gone another seventy-five miles south and had to turn round to try and retrieve my bag. Fortunately it was still there, and Arthur was very kind about it and did not admonish me as I well deserved to be admonished.

Many were the parties we enjoyed with the Barthropps and their friends. Lots of these were famous fighter pilots, and I met many of these gallant men, including perhaps the most gallant of them all: Douglas Bader. Douglas's wife, Thelma, was Arthur's first cousin (as was Thelma's sister, Jill, wife of another famous pilot, Laddie Lucas). Because of this, and because of the Baders' friendship with the Barthropps, I knew the couple well. I have two powerful memories of the man: first of all dancing with him at a Battle of Britain Ball at Grosvenor House – which was not easy, but I felt it was a great privilege. Another, less commendable, occasion occurred at a dinner party in the Barthropps' flat in Eaton Square. Betty had made a delicious avocado mousse as a starter. When Douglas tasted it he screwed up his face and said, 'What is this filthy stuff?! I can't eat it, sorry!' and he pushed his plate away. The next course was fillet of beef fondue, and Betty warned us all not to put the serving forks into our mouths. Either Douglas didn't hear her, or he ignored her advice, and he burnt his mouth quite badly. He *exploded*, shouting at Betty that she was *stupid* to serve such food. Paddy was angry, naturally, and told Douglas that if he was going to be so rude to Betty he'd better fuck off. Which he did; dragging poor Thelma with him. When, a few years later, the Baders had dinner with us in our Barnes cottage, Douglas behaved impeccably!

While Arthur was still married we couldn't, of course, go on holidays together as he had to join his family on trips to Spain and Portugal. The first year that this happened Arthur asked me if I would look after Morgan, his corgi, while he was away. In return he lent me his little grey Mini van, so that year I was able to motor up to Scotland instead of travelling by train. By that time, work on dualling the carriageway of the A1 had nearly finished. Approaching Wetherby, I happened to be bombing along a dualled section at about 70mph and passing everything in the inside lane, when I noticed a police car coming up in the distance behind me. I dutifully pulled over to allow it to pass me – but no; it started flashing its lights to indicate that I should stop. When I had done so, a nice policeman came to my window and asked me if this was my van.

I said it wasn't, it had been lent to me. He asked me if I knew the registration number and I said I didn't. He then asked me whether I knew that vans were restricted to 30mph (which they were in 1960). 'No! Are they really?' Obviously Arthur had never thought to tell me this! The nice policeman then asked me where I was heading and I said 'Inverness'. 'Right, young lady,' said he. 'Thirty miles an hour all the way then ... ' They followed me for a few miles and then peeled off into the town, so I was able to put my foot down again.

As the journey from London to Kincraig was such a long one in a Mini van, I had decided to spend a night somewhere in the border country. Passing through some Forestry Commission country I spotted a track into a wood that looked promising. I found a nice little glade, had some coffee and sandwiches and bedded down with the dogs in the back of the van. I didn't sleep a wink. There were strange animal noises and crackings of twigs and I was terrified. However, I did feel refreshed by the time dawn broke and was soon on my way north again.

By the following year's trip to Speyside I'd been able to purchase my first brand new Mini, YTL 362 – surf blue with surf blue upholstery; it was the prettiest car I could have found.

Weekends, too, were fraught – but Arthur usually managed to get away from the marital home at Little Chalfont to a phone box to ring me, on the pretext that he needed to buy some cigarettes or walk Morgan. Some weekends Arthur would say he had to work, and then we'd be able to get away to friends; in particular to Sammy (Shrimp) and Pam Osborne, old RAF friends who lived in a thatched cottage in West Wittering, next door to the former house of Mr Royce of Rolls Royce, and often down to Herefordshire to visit Pam and Jimmy.

There were many, many dramas, many good things and many bad things before Arthur moved into Cornwall Gardens with me and eventually got his divorce. It was a cliffhanger, because his decree absolute was only granted on the day before our wedding, planned for the 20th August 1966. Even then a mad dash across

Above: Granny with Daddy and Lirlie at Kilmacolm ca 1907.
Below: Dai Todd, Granny and 'Gag-Gag', Bridge of Weir air raid wardens.

Daddy as a bachelor before leaving for India.

Mummy aged 20. This photo was taken on her engagement to Daddy.

Top: Granny and
Gag-Gag Auld.

Above: Me and my sister.

Left: Me aged about 2.

Above: The Grumble Box, probably at the Keelan House in Allahabad.

Below: Lionel Carey and 'Uncle' Mary's reception at The Grange.
Libby Parry-Jones, Trish Barlow and me.

Top left: Me, Hove, 1945.

Top right: Mummy, fag in hand, Woolwich.

Bottom left: Daddy, mounted, ready to lead the
                  Woolwich march past for Princess Margaret.

Bottom right: Mummy, Daddy and me – off to a
                  Buckingham Palace Garden Party, 1949.

This photograph of me was taken to celebrate the success
of my plastic surgery in 1954.

Top left: Ascot 1959. Jack Gerber, Suzanne, John Huston and me.

Top right: My Christmas card, 1959, featuring my Corgi, Tina.

Bottom left: Notleys on the Serpentine: Trevor Cox (William Trevor),
Marissa Martelli, Assia Wevill, Sean Gallagher.

Arthur in his prime.

Arthur and Jane, Hyde Park Hotel, 20th August 1966.

Top left: John Hollington in his 4.5 litre Bentley.

Top right: The shop and house at Melbury, 1969.

Bottom left: New Year's Eve, Colchester Club. Heather, Rees, me, John Hollington.

Bottom right: Mosquito (Fluffy Boy!)

Above: Old Mill House, Wix.

Below: My father with his sisters Mary and Lirlie (my godmother).

Jane and the Stampe at Avranches, France.

Martin in his role as a Lysander pilot.

Above: Martin and me
        with Freddie
        and Max, two
        of Martin's
        grandsons.

Below: Dressed for
        my 70th
        birthday party.

With Auberon Waugh in my garden, 1999.

London was entailed to collect the paperwork needed by the Registrar before he could marry us. Mummy was panic-stricken, but it was decided that in the event of the papers not coming in time we would carry on with the reception as if the marriage had already taken place, and then marry as soon as possible afterwards. Paddy provided a chauffeured Rolls Royce to drive us to Kensington Registry Office and on to the reception at the Hyde Park Hotel. It was only a very small party, as Mummy still disapproved of me marrying an already twice-married man. Pam and Jimmy James, my favourite aunt and uncle, could not be there as they were unable to get anyone to man their village shop in Herefordshire. Betty and Paddy attended, of course, and Shrimp and Pam Osborne, Arthur's daughter Sally and her husband Dermot, and Carol and Robin all managed to be there. The most valued guest was my Great Aunt Mabel, aged 91, who had travelled up from Letchworth by train and taxi to be with us. As a wedding present she gave me the brooch she had been given when bridesmaid to Granny and Gag-Gag on the 1st November 1901. Mabel was the widow of Barry Parker, one of the architects of Letchworth Garden City, the first new town in England. Their house in Letchworth is now a museum devoted to the founding and development of the town.

The sun shone down on us – August 20th 1966 was recorded as the hottest day of that year.

After changing in Mummy and Daddy's bedroom at the hotel, we whizzed back to the flat to collect the dogs before going down to a secret retreat in Wiltshire, but no – before we had downed some more champagne and were about to leave, who should suddenly ring the doorbell but Pam and Sammy, bearing their wedding gift of cut-glass whisky tumblers. So glasses were again raised, and then we set off westwards, with Morgan and Tina on the back seat of Arthur's pale-blue Triumph 2000. We arrived in time for dinner with our hosts, a retired brigadier and his wife, who did posh bed and breakfast in their large country house. The food was fantastic, sparkling were the candles and delicious were the wines. And so to bed, married at last!

Two weeks after our wedding we took off to Scotland for our honeymoon. It was a somewhat unusual honeymoon. I'd seen an advertisement in the *Sunday Times* for a large house to let close to Forres in Inverness-shire. The description was mouth-watering. Sanquhar House had at least six bedrooms, a ballroom and a big drawing room with an open fire and several comfy sofas and chairs. The house belonged to Sheena Mackintosh and her husband. Sheena was the first British woman to win an Olympic Gold Medal for skiing – her actual medal was framed and hung in the downstairs cloakroom, together with many photographs taken at the time. We had decided to have a large house party by way of our honeymoon. Arthur's children, Charles and Alison – then about 15 and 14 respectively – would be coming with us, so we thought it would be nice to invite my favourite aunt, Pamela, her husband Jimmy and their two children, Nicholas and Victoria, who were the same ages as Charles and Ali. We also invited my mother and father. Everyone brought their dogs too, so we had three corgis, a black labrador and a pug to complete the party. The ballroom came into its own when we invited the whole Carey house party from Kincraig over for an evening party in the ballroom, although we only had a wind-up gramophone providing the music. William Carey had just passed his driving test and was acting as chauffeur to the Morven party – who had a fairly terrifying drive back to Kincraig, William still being pretty inexperienced and having partaken generously of the grain.

Sanquhar House had extensive grounds, including a lake and a walled garden with greenhouses bursting with fruit – raspberries, peaches, plums and nectarines. Such a honeymoon involved a lot of work for me, cooking all the meals and shopping for food. A daily cleaner was provided within the rent, and there was a dishwasher, which helped a bit, but by the time I got back to work I was fairly exhausted. My colleagues all teased me, saying I was tired due to my husband's passionate demands – but he was not the culprit. The holiday was a huge success and was talked about for many years to come.

For about a year we had squashed ourselves into the Cornwall

Gardens flat, so Arthur had to leave most of his things in Paddy's Belgravia flat over the Belgravia Car Hire garage. At the time I was working at a dreadful agency, whose offices were in Fleet Street, right between the *Telegraph* and the *Daily Express*. The boss was a horrible man; he used to buy tights, which he'd offer to the office girls, provided they tried them on in his room to make sure they were a good fit. It was here that I managed the Fenwick, Bally Shoes and Frank Usher accounts. I was kept extremely busy and often had to stay working very late – particularly after the boss decided he could no longer afford to pay for my secretary, whom he had decided to make redundant. Working with me, as Art Director, was a great friend in waiting – Roy Reynolds. Roy was an extremely talented artist, with many commissions for portraits of people and animals. He was commissioned by the Duke of Edinburgh to produce paintings of his collection of miniature ponies and by the Shah of Persia to paint many of his native country's animals and birds. Among his most interesting achievements was a mural for the Bulldog Bar & Chophouse of the new Royal Garden Hotel in Kensington – and I was extremely honoured when he gave me, as a wedding present, his rough sketch of two bulldogs, of which I am very fond. Later he was to assist the police by making sketches from descriptions of the IRA Guildford bombers. He had to go into hiding for a time in a remote farmhouse in Herefordshire to escape the threats being made on his life by the (allegedly!) guilty terrorists.

Parking had by then become a nightmare in London, with meters everywhere. I was usually able to find a place in a square alongside St Bride's Church, but every two hours I had to move the car. If I got to work early enough I could sometimes park up by Smithfield Market, where parking was free, but viciously fought over. Thankfully, not long after marrying, I was 'head-hunted' by Tom Robertson, a former director of Notley's who now had an agency of his own – George Cuming in Bond Street – so I was able to tell the boss to stuff it and to move to a happier working environment. Cumings was directly opposite the offices of Elizabeth Arden, with the red door. Gossard, Bear Brand, a Courtauld's fibre called Sarille, Optilon Zips and TAP Portuguese Airways were among the accounts I handled for the last couple of years of my advertising career. It had been an amazingly enjoyable time of my life, and in lots of ways I was sad to give it up.

By 1967 we really had outgrown the flat and were searching for a house. We looked at various mews properties and small houses in Kensington, Fulham and Chelsea – lots of them were very attractive, but all had snags. One day Arthur phoned me at work and said he'd found the perfect property – 80 Lillian Road, in Barnes. It was in a sweet little row of artisans' cottages built around the turn of the century by a prospective builder who named the three little streets of his development after his three daughters – Lillian, Mabel and Fanny. Later on the residents of Fanny asked for their road to be re-named as they were always teased about it.

We found 80 Lill' adorable. It had a tiny garden at the front and a narrow strip of garden at the back. The two downstairs rooms had been made into one and there was a small kitchen with French windows into the garden, plus a horribly cold downstairs bathroom. Upstairs there were three bedrooms. At the time we moved in, the new St Paul's School was being built between our back garden and the river, so it was a dusty summer and meant that our view of the river was partly lost. Next door but one, in the last cottage of the row, lived a retired naval commander and his wife, Hugh and Lydia Haggard – he was a great-nephew of Rider Haggard and he owned first editions of all Haggard's novels. She was a great pianist – playing all the old 1930s and 1940s tunes to which I loved to sing along. We played fun bridge with them and became great friends for the many years before they died.

Living in the house between the Haggards and ourselves was a ghastly couple, whose house and garden were neglected and like a tip, with abandoned lavatories and plumbing equipment. At weekends, when we might be entertaining friends in the garden, they would hang their disgusting washing out on the line, so we decided to erect a fence in order to obscure the eyesores. A couple of days later we found our fence had been pushed over. We immediately replaced it and Arthur proceeded to paint it with Cuprinol. Our furious neighbour came out and tried again to push it down – so Arthur flicked his paintbrush at him and paint splashed onto his washing. The neighbour went berserk and tried viciously to knock the fence down again. Threatened with a call to the police, he eventually calmed down and slunk indoors. Arthur and Hugh were very naughty thereafter; they used to park their cars so they boxed our neighbour in tightly at night, so he'd have to walk to get a bus to his place of work.

Other, more pleasant neighbours included actors Tim West and Prunella Scales. Nearly all the cottages in the lane had been 'gentrified', and in a garage in one of the other roads there was a thriving, cheap and very cheerful bistro serving delicious food, which was much patronised by the locals.

We were pleased when Charles and Alison joined us for a holiday in Ireland. We had decided to hire a VW Camper van and to do a grand tour of both the northern and southern parts of the island. With four passengers, two sets of golf clubs, a tent and three dogs (Alison's miniature long-haired dachshund, Fritzl, came with us) the van was not exactly sprightly and very cramped, but we had good weather and saw lots of scenery – possibly the most spectacular was when we camped for the night in Donegal, on top of the highest cliffs in Ireland – it was awesome. I was terrified that Tina, now fourteen and almost completely blind, would fall over the edge, but all was well.

We spent the first night on Anglesey before crossing from Holyhead to Dun Laoghaire, then went north into Ulster and visited the site of the dreadful Battle of the Boyne. Leaving Donegal, we went to Westport House, then onwards through Galway, Ennis (birthplace of one of my Keelan ancestors), Limerick, Killarney. Nearing Cork, Arthur telephoned an old airforce friend of his, Paddy Bandon – 'The Abandoned Earl' – who lived in a large, very modern bungalow in the grounds of his ruined ancestral home, Bandon Castle, which had been burnt down some years before. We called upon him and his South African wife and admired their all-white standard poodle. There was a story circulated in RAF circles during the war that when Paddy Bandon was stationed in Cairo, he was once visiting a busy hotel in the city and became somewhat hustled as he ascended a wide staircase from the ground floor. He was pushed aside by a man descending the staircase who rudely accosted him, saying: 'Mind where you're going sir – I'm Major the Honourable so-and-so'. To which Paddy replied: 'Well, I've got you on both counts – I'm Group Captain the Earl of Bandon.'!

Unfortunately for Alison and me, Arthur and Charles took every opportunity they could to play a round of golf in lots of the places we visited, leaving us behind to read our books for two or three hours. This was very boring. We did have time to do plenty of sightseeing though, visiting The Ring of Kerry, Cork, Blarney (to kiss the stone), Tipperary, Cashel, Waterford and, finally, Rosslare to catch the ferry back to Fishguard.

I had not been feeling my usual merry self on this holiday, and by the time we got home to Barnes I realised that I was pregnant again. Luckily, by that time there were moves afoot to legalise abortion, and one of the leading gynaecologists of the day, a Mr Diggory, was the consultant at our local hospital in Richmond. He happened to be a leading light in the campaign to change the legislation. I consulted my GP and he referred me to Mr Diggory, whom I was able to convince that I fully deserved a termination because (a) my husband was nearly twenty years older than I, and (b) he was a diabetic and earning only a small salary, which meant I had to earn the bread. We could not possibly afford to keep a child – especially as Charles and Alison were still in their teens and Arthur was supporting them. All went well, and after it was all over I was kitted out with an IUD, which prevented further mishaps.

Chapter Fourteen

Melbury Osmond
(circa 1970)

Deep down in Dorset
Is hidden a village
Hugged among hedgerows
Thickets of brambles
Elder and hazel

Aged oaks shelter her
Elm branches cosset her
Lilac and primrose
Foxglove and cowslip
Flourish; embellish her

Mould'ring leaves lead you there
Far from the highway
Wind you through orchards
And fields full of Fresians
Guernseys and Herefords

Drops the road gently
Winding to watersplash
Cottages cluster

Thatches a'frowning
O'er golden grey stonework
Oak doors shut firmly
Against nosy strangers
A'peeking and prying

Curtains twitch gently
Revealing surveillance
Nothing escaping
Their permanent vigilance
Tireless
Merciless
Ever-defensive

Kittens lie sprawling
Carpeting doorsteps
Teasing and pestering
Snoozing and sucking
Kneading and purring
And cleaning their whiskers

Little old ladies
Wizzened by labouring
Loiter in gateways
Swapping the gossip-snips
Sometimes inventing
Fantasy scandals

Pipe-smoking pensioners
Tending their gardens
Ponder the past
Remember the good days
The courting, the cider
The harvests, the dancing

The girls in frilled petticoats
Winking and teasing them

Now they are old
And their joints often pain them
Their women grow stout
And young girls ignore them
Yet passion still stirs in them

Woodsmoke climbs lazily
Headily scented
From smouldering firesides
Autumn is closing in
Winter approaches
Apples are harvested
Pickles and chutneys
Are stacked into larders

Evening comes early
In byre and barton
Udders are heavy
Ready for milking
Cats seek their saucers
Dogs stretch on hearthrugs
Schoolchildren chatter
Pocket their sherbet and liquorice lovehearts
And slowly stroll homewards

Men shed their muddy boots
Glad the day's over
Throw out their legs
T'wards foot-soothing embers
Snore for a little
While tea is a'brewing

When the moon rises
Shutters are fastened
Flickering candles
Ascend winding stairways
Soft fluffy featherbeds
Fresh with sweet linen
Scented with lavender
Lacily bolstered
Warmly embrace
Their flannel-clad sleepers

Stars twinkle high
Like a flarepath to Heaven
As night settles down
Over woodland and stream
The dead are alive in Eternity's darkness
And Melbury Osmond is only a dream

Jane Donaldson
1970

Arthur's job at that time was secretary to the Hotel & Catering Trades Benevolent Association, which as well as being poorly paid was pretty boring. I, too, was getting tired of my job and the drive to work entailing queuing to get over Hammersmith Bridge and back each day in rush hour traffic, together with parking restrictions getting fiercer and fiercer. Having spent so many wonderful weekends with Pam and Jimmy James at their shop near Leominster, we began to think we might do the same and leave London for the West Country. And so the search for a suitable shop began. It was fun visiting the many properties we inspected. We had been sent particulars of several shops and post offices in East Devon and Dorset and we set off to visit one or two of them. One shop, in the village of Melbury Osmond a few miles south of Yeovil, sounded a bit grand for us and we nearly decided not to look at it. It claimed to have five bedrooms, a swimming pool and an orchard with a trout stream, as well as a stable and other outbuildings. However, after spending a night at The Acorn in Evershot we decided we'd have a look at it. It was love at first sight. We offered the full asking price, about £12,000, and set the legals in motion next day. Arthur had very little money, just his pension, so with help from my godmother, Aunt Lirlie, I managed to get a mortgage. I was now well on the property ladder; the flat had cost £2,500 and sold for £4,000, 'Lill' Road' cost about £5,500 and sold for £7,500 (in just over a year – but we had made a few minor improvements and had completely re-decorated). A lot of people came to view the Barnes house, but it was a long time before anyone actually made us an offer. Meanwhile, completion date arrived for the purchase of The Post House – or 'Po Ho' as it came to be known. We knew it would be difficult to sell Lill' Road without its furniture and curtains, so we decided to take camp beds and other basic necessities with us and move to Melbury regardless, leaving the agents to earn their commission by selling 80 Lillian Road.

On Wednesday the 30th August we set off for Dorset in two cars, Arthur with Morgan and Ali in his newly purchased Triumph 2.5 PI, Tina and myself in my Mini – the cars were a matching pair, maroon with fawn upholstery – planning to race each other to Dorset. We had arranged to overlap a couple of days with the outgoing family, the Waters, to liaise with them so they could show us the ropes in the shop. Mr Waters was an ex-Rhodesian policeman and the couple had two sons, both of whom were at Sherborne Grammar School. We arrived at the shop soon after three to find everyone in a flap because the post office in Dorchester said they couldn't do the handover on Friday. However, I telephoned them and managed to sort it out. We didn't do a lot of 'learning' in the shop that day, so we went off to the pub in Chetnole, a neighbouring village, to try and get fixed up for the night. While we were there we saw and reserved a delicious little black and white kitten! There was no room at that inn, so we went back to The Acorn where we arranged to stay the night, all three of us and the dogs in one bedroom. We then whizzed off to Yeovil and had a Chinese dinner.

Next day Jean Waters took us in to Yeovil and introduced us to the meat wholesaler and to a vast warehouse, Budgets, the cash and carry. When we got back to Melbury with a picnic lunch, who should turn up just as we were finishing it but Paddy and Betty Barthropp in their Rolls Royce PPB 1 – Betty very glamorous in a pink trouser suit. They loved the house and garden and were amazed by the swimming pool!

The swimming pool was not an off-the-peg pool. It had been dug out by a local builder and lined with pale-blue concrete. The filter system was extremely primitive; water was pumped up from the deep end to a fountain, which fell into an old iron tank filled with small gravel chips before draining back into the shallow end of the pool. It all worked perfectly.

After the Barthropps had left, we followed Douglas Waters on his delivery round to familiarise ourselves with the route. We then dined and slept again at The Acorn. Here are two extracts from my diaries of the time:

Thursday 1st August
Got up to a bright but misty morning and the sun never really put in an appearance. We went into Yeovil. Ali and I bought paper knickers! We hung about in the garden for most of the day, as Pickfords were there packing up the Waters' things. My cooker arrived, so I produced spag bol for all of us for dinner. The garden looked lovely and I couldn't stop walking round the house, looking into every empty room and trying to get used to the fact that it all belongs to ME AND ARTHUR!

Friday 2nd August
In the morning the training officer, a young woman, came and began the task of teaching me the post office bit. The Waters left at about six, after we'd pushed and shoved their

caravan out of the back gate. We then went and collected our little black and white kitten from the Chetnole pub. He is divine, and so good, settling in with us straight away. We have decided to call him Tesco (because we are now grocers) Acorn (after the pub) Chetnole (because he was born there).

Meanwhile, we were still camping out, waiting to sell 80 Lill', so all our things were still in Barnes, when the following Sunday I had a phone call from my sister Carol (she and her husband Robin happened to be at Wix that weekend) to say that Daddy was in Colchester Military Hospital having had a heart attack, that he was very ill and she thought I should come quickly. I immediately rushed back in my Mini to Colchester to find Daddy in bed and looking as white as a sheet, with an oxygen mask on his face. He seemed really happy to see me, and I think he was very relieved that I had managed to get there in time, because at 8 p.m. that evening, as we sat down to dinner, the hospital phoned to say Daddy had peacefully died, after another heart attack. For Daddy, his going could not have been better timed. He had just returned from four days' sailing in the North Sea with his two greatest friends, 'Squirrel' McKay Lewis and Alec Grieve. They had enjoyed a wonderful sail; they'd drunk a lot of whisky and they'd sung songs to the accompaniment of Squirrel's banjo – but Daddy had felt very tired by the time he got home and had taken to his bed. Mummy had been very alarmed and called the doctor, who imme-diately had Daddy moved to hospital. Some time after his funeral, as he would have wished I'm sure, Squirrel and Alec took whisky and banjo out to sea and ceremonially ditched Daddy's ashes into the North Sea.

This was not the only drama that occurred that weekend while I was away. Arthur and Ali were alone at Melbury, of course, having to run the shop themselves. Fortunately the lady from the post office would be there on the Monday, and Mrs Groves, who used to help the Waters in the shop, could be called upon to assist. The very same evening that we got the bad news from the hospital, Arthur rang us at Wix in a real state to say that there was a herd of cows in the garden and two of them had fallen into the swimming pool! He was told who the likely owner was by villagers and phoned the farmer who, with a couple of lads to help and with the aid of Morgan – a proper cattle-herding corgi! – the cows were rescued. Of course, the pool then had to be drained and scrubbed, and by the time I was able to return home all was back to normal again, the hole in the hedge having already been repaired.

To complicate things further, we were at last due to complete the sale of 80 Lillian Road and had arranged for Pickfords to move our things to Dorset during the week following Daddy's death. Of course Carol and I could not leave Mummy to do all the funeral arrangements etc. and I had already planned to finish the packing-up in Barnes in good time for the move. This was now impossible. Pickfords were brilliant. They said they were used to such dramas and they could cope by themselves with packing everything up, including our clothes and stuff in the kitchen as well.

Poor Mummy was absolutely devastated by Daddy's death. Since he had come back from the war he had taken over all the paying of bills and the general administrative side of the household. Mummy was brilliant about running the domestic side of things, and she could turn her hand to decorating and organising their busy social life. She had been incredibly strong during the war, coping with finding places for us to live once the army quarters were no longer available, as well as dealing with my schools' repeated reports of my intolerable behaviour, but she had by now come to rely on him much more than in previous years. She tried to be brave, but it was a battle for her. Wix became too much for her to cope with alone, what with the garden, the vegetable garden and taking on total responsibility for running Old Mill House. She moved to a smaller, modern house in Colchester off Lexden Road, and then to a ground-floor flat in a pretty Georgian villa nearby in Lexden. She still had the last-surviving member of our corgi family, Meg, and a ginger kitten, Simba, which we had given her from a litter born on a

Melbury farm – from where we, too, had acquired three ginger kittens, Sainsbury, Waitrose and Lipton (the latter to become known, for reasons yet to be explained, as 'Tiger Lipton Jack'). Mummy did drive down to visit us at Melbury a couple of times, but once she no longer drove we didn't see her in Melbury again.

My mother really no longer had a life – only an existence. Her next move was to very pleasant sheltered accommodation in Petersfield, Hampshire, to be near to my sister who lived up the hill in Steep. Then even that became too much for her and she had to move in to a care home. She was, for a time, able to continue with her cigarettes and nightly tots of whisky, but as dementia began to take hold even those pleasures were removed from her. Mummy had for many years been a sixty-a-day smoker, but she was beginning to get careless with her cigarettes, and once she nearly set fire to her room – so no more fags. Eventually she had to be moved to a proper nursing home. It was very well run by Roman Catholics, who cared for her in a kind manner. She had a pleasant little room with patio doors opening onto a beautiful garden. By now, she did not even recognise me when I visited – so I'm afraid my visits became fewer and fewer and the burden of visiting fell completely onto my sister's shoulders. Mummy died in 2000, aged ninety.

When we lived at Melbury we had a ginger striped cat that we at first called Lipton – which inevitably metamorphosed into 'Tiger' because he looked like one! From the beginning Lipton was 'different'. He had a habit, when he wanted attention, of standing on his hind legs and scraping at the kitchen cabinets, making a fearsome noise until one made a fuss of him or gave him some food. Also, like some dogs, if you held your arms out wide he would *leap* from a standing start vertically up and land on your chest. He was particularly devoted to Arthur and spent most of our telly-watching time in Arthur's arms.

The second of the three airforce Donaldson brothers, John William (also known as 'Baldy' or 'Jack'), was famous for landing his squadron of Gladiators on a frozen lake in the north of Norway at the time that country was fighting against occupation by Germany. When retreat was inevitable he led his squadron to make successful deck landings on HMS *Glorious*. Tragically, the ship was torpedoed and sunk. Jack was drowned.

Arthur began to comment, quite soon after Tiger became an adult cat, that his character was much like Jack's. Then, when Arthur's brother Teddy and his wife Anne-Sofie arrived to spend Christmas with us in 1971, Tiger went quite mad. He ran in circles round Teddy and, quite literally, gave us an aerobatic display from the back of a sofa, leaping in the air and doing slow-rolls (or rather fast ones). It was really uncanny. He also had an unpleasant habit of disappearing, sometimes for a couple of days, sometimes for two or three weeks at a time. We would go out looking for him and calling his name – then suddenly, often more than half a mile away from home and out of the densest thicket or wood, he would appear, and after a lot of tempting would allow himself to be carried home. Sometimes we could not find him – but when he felt it was time he would return home and show unbridled affection for us – particularly for Arthur. I kept a log of his longer disappearances, and some of the dates he chose were very, very strange:

1974–5
Tiger went away on December 31st and came back on January 9th (Arthur's birthday).

He went away on June 8th (the anniversary of the sinking of HMS *Glorious*) and he came home at 10 p.m. on the 29th June (Jack/Baldy's birthday).

On September 14th or 15th he left for the last time. We found him nearly a mile away from home (the forester had told his wife, who was my daily help, that he'd seen a ginger cat dead in the woods and described his position). On the 20th we found him, soaking wet, in grass and bracken. He'd obviously been dead a couple of days. We took him to the vet, not for a post mortem but just to be examined. The vet said that Tiger had died of pneumonia *and his lungs were full of water.* Strange!

After Arthur's mother, Granny Donaldson, died, I designed and made two kneelers for Melbury Church. One featured a hedgehog (because her nickname was Mrs Tiggywinkle) with some tiny daffodils (her favourite flowers) and the initials 'GMD', the other a ginger cat with the RAF wings. There are also photos of Arthur and Tiger fast asleep in bed together and captioned 'The Brothers'.

Chapter Fifteen

Once everything had settled down again we concentrated on being grocer and sub-postmistress and getting to know our customers. There was an awesome lot to be learnt. Serving the customers and re-filling shelves was the easy part. Becoming expert at buying was much more difficult. Sometimes we'd run out of things and often we would buy too much. A lot of the time we fed on out-of-date items like sausages with fur on them, stale bread and cakes, past-it fruit and vegetables etc. Of course the post office was a nightmare once the three-week training period was over. There was so much paperwork, and the dreadful task every Friday evening of trying to balance the books. Every stamp and postal order had to be counted, cash had to be reconciled, every pension docket had to be bundled up for return. Once I had acquired an adding machine the situation eased a bit, but until then I had to add everything up myself – and I have always been hopeless at arithmetic. It was very rare for the result to be a perfect reconciliation, but I soon learnt to massage the final figures either up or down, depending on the actual difference – which was never very much, but it was a frustration to fail. When we became 'decimalised', adding up was a lot easier.

Gradually we got the hang of things and established a routine whereby I concentrated on stock control and did the weekly trip to the cash and carry and Arthur excelled himself serving the customers and doing the weekly deliveries round in the village and to several surrounding farms. Mrs Groves helped us in the shop on busy days and we had other occasional helpers too, which enabled us to get away for long weekends and short weekday breaks. It was easy enough to deal with the balancing up of the post office on a Thursday or a Monday instead.

While the Waters family kept the shop, they kept a meticulous record of all that they took from it for themselves. We were completely free and easy and just used it as a large larder – and as we had an off-licence as well we just helped ourselves to as much alcohol as we pleased. Of course we were pretty extravagant, and also we entertained lavishly, so our accounts showed very poor figures. When decimalisation came in we coped quite well, but I had to go on a Post Office course in Dorchester.

Arthur was known as 'Arthur', 'Mr Donaldson' or 'Mr D.' in the shop, although it was common knowledge that he was a retired Group Captain and a much-decorated WW2 fighter ace, because the local newspaper, the *Western Gazette,* had run an article featuring his valiant background and his new venture. One of the previous owners of the shop had been a Squadron Leader, who rather pompously insisted on being addressed by his rank – but a very ancient and characterful customer, Mr Curtis, a gnarled and rustic old fellow who used to lean against the counter smoking a roll-up and gossiping with Arthur, told him that he had been admonished by the said Squadron Leader for not using his rank – to which mischievous Mr Curtis replied, 'I'll call YOU Squadron Leader if you'll call ME Driver Curtis!' He had served in the First World War. Mrs Curtis was tiny, and she didn't have a tooth in her head, but she loved to talk and would lean against the counter chatting, and when she laughed you could see all her gums.

The village was a cauldron of characters and some of them used very funny words when asking for things: 'kennel meat', 'squeaky bacon', 'Typhoon tea', 'curly butter', 'mangle chutney'. For some extraordinary reason many of our female customers liked to share their secrets and worries with Arthur. Their ailments were described in lurid detail. One woman – and she was a highly educated one – who incidentally did not marry until she was fifty, complained that she was having to go to the doctor because she was suffering from 'dry vagina'. She also described her urine, which was cloudy and full of pus. Yuk, yuk, yuk! Even worse, when on one occasion she was constipated, she told Arthur that when her bowels did open she passed stools 'twelve inches long and two inches thick'!

Another lady, the widow of quite a senior soldier, frequently gave Arthur details of her attacks of diarrhoea. Arthur took it all in his stride and made soothing noises, but when it came to the woman who told him she had 'piles like bunches of grapes' he found it difficult not to giggle. The last, and most revolting, confidence he was expected to share was that of a woman with a bad cold who was 'bringing up green phlegm'. She also said she was suffering from 'bicycle-seat cystitis' and felt all hot and sweaty.

I have not made up these incidents – I promise you. I made notes of them at the time in my diaries!

One of our best customers was Miss Flatman, daughter of a former estate gamekeeper – or *was* she his daughter? Village gossip had it that she was the product of a liaison between her mother and the Earl of that time. Certainly she had been given a good education, and she had a few fine pieces of furniture and pictures in her cottage (although she still didn't have an indoor lavatory!). She was now a mistress at the village school and she was a great personality. She had a man in her life, Dick House, but he did not live with her because he had a mentally disabled brother who needed looking after, but he visited regularly and they used to go to Taunton and Wincanton races together. Sadly, he was killed in an accident on the main Dorchester road, and his invalid brother had to be put into a home.

Thursday October 8th
We went to Dick House's funeral today. It was like a biblical multitude. I have never seen so many at a funeral. About seventy-five of us could not get into the church and had to

stand outside. Esmée was so brave and composed. She stood waiting by the gate as we all arrived. Of course the Alliance lorry (our wholesaler's delivery vehicle) arrived at just the wrong time and could not get any further than the top of the hill because of all the parked cars. After much manoeuvring (which we witnessed from the churchyard), the lorry managed to pull over enough to allow the hearse to squeeze by, but it meant a long delay. The driver was very patient and understanding and we gave him a cup of tea and a good tip later. Being outside the church was less harrowing than being inside – one did not feel quite so involved.

The headmaster of the school was Mr Dewey, a quiet, well-mannered man with a rather noisy and boisterous wife. They lived in Sterndale Cottage, into which, after their retirement from the village, settled Arthur's mother, 'Granny Donaldson', for the last few years of her life.

There were two vets in the village, which was very fortunate as we frequently consulted them, with our four cats and two dogs. Once, Tesco was caught up by a verge trimmer. He very bravely dragged himself home across a meadow, although half his coat was hanging off and one ear was badly torn. We threw him into our Mini van and rushed him up to the surgery, where the vet, Bob Oaksford, stitched him up – he used forty-five sutures, but Tesco was none the worse once he'd healed.

Melbury Osmond was still almost feudal in 1969. The Vicarage and The Post House were the only freeholds in the village; all the other properties were owned by the Ilchester Estate and most housed estate workers or pensioners. Melbury House itself was surrounded by parkland, with lakes and ponds and ancient trees. In the early days of living there one was allowed to walk in the park freely, although driving through it to get to the Acorn Inn in Evershot, the larger village also part of the estate, was benevolently frowned upon. On the death of the last Earl, there was no direct male heir to inherit the title, which passed to a group captain in the Royal

Air Force, but Melbury House and the estate, together with considerable other lands in Dorset, as well as large areas of Holland Park in London, benefitted a daughter, married to Lord Galway, whose family owned many acres of coal-rich land in Yorkshire. We saw little of her ladyship, but her young daughter, Charlotte, would often ride her pony into the village to come and buy ice creams.

By the time Charlotte came to inherit, which she did at a young age, times had changed, and the relaxed attitude to running the Melbury Estate had to change too. A racehorse-breeding stud was set up, and many valuable mares were kept on the estate. We could no longer wander where we pleased and were supposed to keep to the public footpaths – and of course our breakfast-picnics cooked on little fires came to a stop.

We soon got to know some of the locals. First to call on us were Jock and Eileen Henderson, who ran the village stores in Yetminster – a neighbouring village. They didn't live over the shop but in a handsome old rectory in the next village, Ryme Intrinseca. There were two Jock Hendersons in Ryme: the keeper of the Yetminster shop and a retired Bishop of Bath and Wells. They lived directly opposite each other. We also met friends of theirs, Robert and Norah White, who lived in a large house in Yetminster, Gable Court. The Whites had two grown-up sons: Daniel, who lived in Scotland, and Patrick, who worked on the Baltic Exchange in London. Robert had a small engineering firm near Yetminster railway station. One of his friends/clients was Lord Strathcona, whose vintage Mercedes car was kept in the Gable Court garage and the family was free to use it. Daniel in particular took it out for a run whenever he could manage to get down from Glasgow.

We'd only been in Dorset for about a year when Robert White had a terrible accident. He was driving a sit-on mower, preparing the village cricket pitch for the annual match always arranged by Daniel and Patrick, with a team of Patrick's smart London friends pitted against Daniel's team of country bumpkins. Suddenly the mower tipped over on top of Robert. He was dreadfully shocked, although not actually badly injured. The following morning Norah woke up to find Robert dead in bed, having suffered a massive heart attack. Norah never really recovered from the event. We'd had many good times with the two of them, enjoying dinners and occasionally playing bridge together. The immediate problem that had to be addressed was the future of the engineering business. As Daniel was knowledgeable enough to understand the mechanics and he'd gained experience in public relations while working in Glasgow, it was decided that he should come south again and take over the running of the company. He also had knowledge of the business community in Yeovil, having started training in law at a local solicitors, from which he had been given notice after he was discovered in an inappropriate act in a partner's office during a summer lunch hour. Daniel had been married and had two children, whom he had left behind in Scotland, but by now he was divorced and had a Scottish girlfriend, Vivian Johnston. The plan was that as soon as Daniel was established down in Yetminster and could find somewhere for them to live, Vivian would come and join him down in Dorset.

I well remember my first meeting with Vivian. Jock and Eileen Henderson (the grocers, not the bishop) were hosting the Ryme Intrinseca village fête that summer and on one of the sideshows was a Gentlemen's Knobbly Knees competition, which Vivian was scheduled to judge. She was wearing a floaty summer dress, she was tall and slim and she had long glossy jet-black hair. She obviously enjoyed her task of judging the knees, and there was much laughter and many facetious remarks. I can't remember who won – but it certainly wasn't Arthur.

We both took to Vivian at once and promised her we would put feelers out to find somewhere for her to live. As it happened, it was not long before the cottage next-door to us, Post Office Cottage, became available to rent, and so Vivian came down south and moved in. Between our house and the next door cottage there was a tall laurel hedge, in which there was a small iron gate – so we soon fell into using this gate for going in and out of each others' houses.

Arthur and I had got into the habit of getting up very early and going for leisurely walks through the Melbury Estate and the fields surrounding the village. We'd get back in time to open the shop and we'd devour a good English breakfast to revive us from our exertions. Vivian asked to come too on our walks, so each morning after making coffee I would stagger round to wake her before we set off. Our walks were magic. Not one of the three of us had previously lived in such very rural surroundings, and to walk up little lanes bursting with wild flowers – first snowdrops, then prim-roses, wild iris and daffodils and anemones, followed by cow-parsley, wild garlic and campion was a joyous new experience. Later it was time for blossoming fruit trees and bluebells. As well as all this there were other treats of nature to enjoy. In the mad month of March we witnessed the playful boxing of hares and the chasing circles they performed for us. We also watched the behaviour of piggy-wigs, either snoozing in their corrugated iron 'Nissen huts' or enjoying the early morning sunshine outside. Once we watched the foreplay of a mating pair – no hurried coupling as with dogs and most other animals, but gentle rubbing of noses, snufflings of ears. We were touched – and rather excited at the same time by our voyeurism!

At weekends, when we usually had a houseful of family and friends, we would set out towards our favourite picnicking places, bearing a tin kettle and frying pan, sausages, bacon, mushrooms, eggs and wine, and collect kindling wood to make a fire and have a hilarious brunch, with plenty of wine.

Among our most frequent house-guests were Peter and Annie Horsley. Arthur and Peter had been RAF friends since wartime, when Arthur was Peter's boss and Peter used to make tea for him. Peter was promoted rapidly and became Equerry to HRH Prince Philip at the time of the Coronation and was knighted when he retired as an Air Marshal. Annie had been married previously to another airman, but by then they were divorced, and as soon as Peter was also free from his previous marriage to Phyllis, they were able to marry. Annie had two sons and two daughters. The Horsleys (or the Horseflies as we called them) were huge fun and we enjoyed many parties with them at their series of houses in and near Stockbridge.

Other friends who came to stay were an air marshall and his wife, Christopher and Joan Foxley Norris. They had a psychic experience when they slept in the guest room that overlooked the garden and swimming pool. Legend had it that this room was haunted. Joan was suffering from a bad back at the time. During the night she dreamt that her back was being massaged, and when she woke up in the morning her backache had gone! Christopher, one of the wittiest of men, wrote in the visitors' book: 'Three in a bed can be just the most, but not when the third one is some bloody ghost!'.

Arthur's daughter Sally, her husband Dermot, plus their two small girls, Georgina and Arabella, would visit us from London at least once a month – the girls enjoying the houseful of animals, and playing in the orchard and outhouses among the Maran hens, bantams and white doves. Other frequent visitors were Paddy and Betty Barthropp, with whom we often spent weekends in their converted railway station in Devon, Hatherleigh Halt.

Another aviator with whom we met up was Mike Fell. He and his wife had a house near Chichester and were friends with the Osbornes (or Osbums as we called them) so we saw them quite frequently on our visits to Selsey and Wittering. Mike had been taught to fly by Arthur in the early 1940s. He was not RAF but Fleet Air Arm, and by the time we caught up with him he was an admiral, living in Naples and captain of HMS *Ark Royal*. Not long after we'd settled in to Melbury he was posted to Yeovilton and provided with a large house in the hamlet of Wales, which his wife Joan had completely redecorated. It was fully staffed with uniformed sailor servants, including an excellent chef. Much entertaining of senior service people, politicians and 'celebs' was part of the job, and we were frequently invited to their dinner parties – sometimes at very short notice to help them to make up numbers.

These were marvellous dinner parties, with stewards in white gloves serving the most delicious food – and finger bowls and vintage port. And Joan's incredible 'surprises' for people's birthdays. Arthur once got a birthday cake with two spitfires made from icing sugar, and I remember 'Killy' Kilmartin being invited for lunch (by chance) on his birthday and arriving to find his old friends Laurie and Daphne Kelly, the Donaldsons and the Barthropps were there as well. Then there was the memorable Air Day, when we were invited to luncheon at Wales House beforehand with all the glittering people. After feeding and wining in the garden on a perfect sunny July Saturday, we were ushered to our cars and detailed as to who should follow whom by police motorcyclists, who escorted us for the couple of miles to the aerodrome, part of the route being on the traffic-clogged A303, at high speed, passing all the other traffic to ensure we were not delayed. Champagne at lunch and strawberries and cream in the Admiral's marquee for tea. Something altogether unforgettable – to say nothing of a truly superb air display!

We met so many famous/infamous people at those Wales House dinners; I once sat next to James Robertson Justice – rude and blustering and thoroughly pleased with himself – and also his nice Estonian wife. Jimmy Edwards – the most boring show-off of all time. Lord Peyton, at that time our local MP and Minister of Transport, who never drove himself and thought that wearing seatbelts should be compulsory. Ugh!

I remember well the big, fat cook and the small, impeccable chief steward, both of whom became almost friends and always recognised and greeted us. And Mike himself, who used to frighten me *silly* at first, but who was always so courtly and flattering. Joan would often seat me on his right when there were much more important people deserving that privilege. How much Arthur and I relished those exotic evenings and relaxed Sunday lunches.

Mike died much too early, as my 1976 diary describes:

4th December 1976
Today it is in the papers that Mike Fell died yesterday, near home and apparently in his car. They'd been up to London

to a dinner and just before reaching home he had collapsed. Joan had to take the wheel and switch off the ignition and pull on the handbrake. Fortunately the car ended up on a grass verge and there was no crash. He died immediately. I have just written my sad letter to Joan.

Mike was not a fit man, of course. For as long as I have known him he has had a terrible cough, and he smoked heavily. Then he had a coronary and was in Midhurst Hospital for several weeks. However, the last time we saw him, at the Osbornes, he looked so much better and so dashing and good-looking.

Back down to earth as grocers, we continued to enjoy both work and play at Po Ho, as The Post House was now generally known. Our family of animals had been added to by a rescue golden labrador bitch, whom we christened 'Sanquhar' after the house of our Scottish honeymoon.

During the summer drought of 1976 we discovered there was a well below our kitchen. One of the village old-timers, a tooth-less old lady called Mrs Gosney, came out with the information that we had the deepest well in the village, which never dried out. She pointed its location out to me and I could see signs of rust showing through the horrible Marley tiles. So I armed myself with hammer and chisel and started hacking away. Not only did I find an iron manhole cover but also after lifting it, I looked down into what looked like a bottomless pit filled halfway up with water. We plumbed and found our well was thirty-five feet deep. We tasted the water and it was delicious and wonderfully cool. The drought meant that we were forbidden to top up the swimming pool, although we did sometimes creep out in the middle of the night and furtively turn on the hosepipe – I was, and still am, 'agin the government'.

Whilst chipping away to open up the well I discovered that beneath the Marley tiles were beautiful flagstones. Single-handedly, I spent most of the rest of the summer and well into winter chipping away until the whole kitchen floor was paved with large rectangular flags. This inspired me to redecorate the kitchen and to build, guided by a do-it-yourself manual, a large dresser-top to house my huge collection of dug-up bottles and jars. I had discovered what was the ancient 'rubbish tip' in our orchard, where I'd uncovered not only old bottles and jars but lots of other treasures: an old iron pig trough, three separate parts of a rusting old Petters pump, brass door-knobs (discarded when previous owners of the house had replaced them with red plastic ones, which I'd already binned and fitted new brass ones instead!), and many, many large pieces of vandalised Art Nouveau tiles as well as pieces of white marble and two perfect marble corbels – these had been cast out when a rather ugly hamstone fireplace was installed in the drawing room.

The summer of the drought was when Arthur suffered his first heart attack. It was very frightening having to dial 999 for the first time in my life and to see him carted off to Yeovil hospital. He was kept in for three weeks before being pronounced fit. At the discharge meeting with his physician he was asked if he had any questions. He replied, 'Yes; what about sex?' To which the doctor said, 'Oh, that's OK – as long as you don't get too excited!'

We had too many excitements to mention them all, but one incident needs to be told. Melbury was in Cattistock country and the hunt was frequently seen in and around the village. One Saturday afternoon we could hear the huntsman's horn sounding rather loudly behind the house. We went to see what was happening, only to discover that the pool (covered not too tightly with plastic for the winter) had four hounds floundering in the water and more hounds following behind. I was fearful that the hounds might drown, so I threw myself into the pool, shoes and all, and lifted four hounds up to the unsaddled huntsman, who by now was getting his pack under control. I never saw the fox who was being chased, but the huntsman told me that he'd gone next door into Vivian's garden and had taken refuge in the woodshed. The kennel-man was then sent for and the fox was 'dispatched'.

That evening the Master of the Hunt called upon us to apologise for the upheaval and promised to replace the damaged plastic pool-cover. A week later I received a Basil Brush tea towel and a follow-up letter of apology. I also got a mention in the Cattistock newsletter:

> The meet at Melbury after the Hunt Ball was a happy occasion on which a very large crowd both mounted and dismounted were entertained by Lady Agnew and Major MacEwan … Hounds then drew Marlpits finding a fox almost at once. They were quickly in difficulty among the gardens of Melbury Osmond. The fox had taken refuge in a woodshed behind the post office. On learning that the postmaster's geese had been lost earlier in the week this fox was accounted for. Extracting the hounds was more hazardous when some of them ran over the polythene cover of a swimming pool. Disaster was prevented by Mrs Donaldson, who waded into the pool and pulled hounds out.

Next morning, a Sunday, we were having a lie-in when the front door bell rang. Arthur went to investigate and our new next-door neighbour asked; 'Is everything all right? We went to fetch some wood in and found the shed was spattered with blood!'. He was obviously afraid that some foul murder had been committed. (By then Vivian had moved from next-door to a larger cottage 'The Nook', just up the hill from us.)

One weekend, Vivian had some friends from Scotland to stay: Jim ('the butcher' – because he was one) and Rosemary Moore. As well as the McDermott family (Sally and her husband and children) we had Peter Vernon (Joanna Bindley's doctor from our days in London) staying with us at the time, without a girlfriend on this occasion. After a very alcoholic lunch indoors Peter took himself upstairs to bed for a nap. The rest of us decided to continue the party down by the stream, taking a couple of two-litre bottles of wine down to keep up our spirits. It was an extremely hot day and everyone started stripping off (except me, of course). When the two bottles of wine had been downed, more wine was called for, and Jim, by now stark-bollock naked, offered to do the necessary. He staggered across the stream and through the orchard – in full view of the family living in the next-door field – before triumphantly returning with yet another bottle.

We were enjoying such happy times then, with masses of visitors to stay and parties galore. But our bank manager was becoming more and more disagreeable. He told us we were living well above our means and told us we had to reduce our borrowings drastically. What a horrible thought ...

Chapter Sixteen

We employed a Yeovil firm of accountants to produce our annual tax returns. We liked the person who looked after our affairs and became friendly with him and his wife. To begin with the friendship was not a particularly close one, but we played bridge together and would dine and have enjoyable evenings. When VAT was about to be introduced, I had a letter from this accountant suggesting that we should have a meeting in his office so he could explain the various options of dealing with the change in the way I kept the books. I thought this was a sensible idea and an appointment was made. When I was ushered into his office I naturally took a seat on a chair across the desk from him. 'Don't sit there,' he said. 'Come round and sit beside me, it will be easier to explain things'. In all innocence I acquiesced. He sat himself very close to me and I thought this was a little strange – but, to my shame, I found it was rather pleasant. We dealt with the question of VAT and then had a coffee and a general chat. Nothing was said about the pleasure of sitting so closely beside each other – but the atmosphere was rather definitely charged.

From that day onwards our bridge evenings became opportunities for surreptitious and intoxicating flirtation.

Although we were living way, way above our means, we had managed somehow to pacify the beastly bank manager for several years, but we were making larger and larger losses. The only way to keep our heads above water seemed to be that I should get a job. Of course there was no chance of getting work in advertising or PR in the backwoods of the West Country, so I fell back on my secretarial training and had no difficulty in finding work in Yeovil with Aviation & Helicopter Sales – which dealt in spares for helicopters and was thus closely involved with Westlands. Working full time, I was now free at lunchtime, and it was not long before my accountant was on the phone inviting me out for lunch with him. These meetings became more and more frequent, and when summertime came we no longer lunched in pubs but took picnics and wine out into secret rural hideaways.

Meanwhile, life at Po Ho was becoming increasingly fraught. It was a great strain working full time and yet having to look after the stock levels and ordering in the shop. Although Arthur did a great job in selling to the customers, he would be careless about keeping things tidy. In particular, when the frozen-food supplier made his delivery he would simply open the freezer lid and dump the new delivery on top of the old stock. I would have to sort all that out when I got home from work. I then had to cook the dinner – and it was all becoming a bit too much for me. As well as that, we were still entertaining a lot, which meant even more work for me. Hardest of all were the regular McDermott weekends.

At one point Sally asked if they could come to stay for three weeks in August so the children could get away from London in their summer holiday. Of course I said they could come. Dermot said I would not have to worry about organising dinners and they would either take us out or Sally would cook. For a few days that worked, but soon I got no help from them at all. I could take no more. I phoned the Barthropps, whom I knew were staying down at their old railway station at Hatherleigh, and invited myself to stay with them for the weekend. I told no one at home – I simply left a note on the kitchen table saying I'd had enough. I just wanted to get away and let them manage without me. I packed a small case and hid it behind the dining room curtains while I went to get the Mini van round to the front ready for my getaway. I don't know how Arthur guessed that I was up to something, but he did. A terrible row ensued, but I was just able to get away from him and drive off in the Mini. Of course I could not manage to retrieve my case from the dining room, so I left without anything – no toothbrush, no make-up, no hairbrush, no change of clothing. Nothing. I had to stop off in Exeter to buy everything from scratch. Safely installed at the railway station, and with an enormous whisky in my hand, I regaled my troubles to Betty and Paddy. They cheered me up by telling me that that we were all going out to dinner with their old friends Brian and Lesley Kingcombe, as it was Lesley's birthday. Just as we were setting off there was a roaring of a motor and a screeching of brakes and Arthur drove up to the house. He had given immediate chase after I left. I absolutely refused his pleas to allow him to stay and join the party and sent him packing back to Melbury. In retrospect I felt very mean about the whole affair, but I had suffered monumental provocation. I had to get back to work on the Monday, so we all managed to simmer down and try to forget what had happened. But it was one of many upsetting things that were pushing me more and more into the affair that was to bring thunderclouds to the idyllic sun-filled life we had enjoyed for nearly ten years in Melbury.

Anger was boiling up inside me, adding to the stress of our worsening financial position. I decided there was nothing for it but to sell a few of my precious dog pictures. My diary of the 20th November 1976 reveals my feelings at that time:

I have a horrid and very frightening fear that today could be a sort of watershed in my life. I have parted, and it has been a painful and sad parting, with four of my favourite dog pictures.

I have been building my collection since early in the 1960s and it has meant a lot to me. I bought each one because I loved it and needed it – it was almost like giving a lonely dog a home in every case. I had not bought any more since coming to Melbury because I no longer had the money to indulge myself.

I have been in a 'state' since I woke this morning; dreading the arrival of the Bonhams man. The pictures sat in the hall, like passengers in transit in some surrealist airport lounge. Uncle Tom's Wife (it's a copy of a Landseer's *Uncle Tom and His Wife For Sale*) shivered apprehensively beside her mate, who sat bravely with his chin held high as if to reassure her that he would take care of her whatever fate held in store for them. The King Charles spaniels (another Landseer copy) just waited patiently for a new owner. The two Armfield paintings of frisky terriers just waited.

The shop closed and Arthur came to cook his lunch. In his usual hopeless fashion he could not find the cutlery (I was in the process of building the kitchen dresser at the time) and he became annoyed. So I snapped at him a bit when I replied that it was at the bottom of the four-drawer pile. This provoked a fiery loud-mouthed attack and a slammed door. I tried to explain that I thought it was mean of him always to get annoyed at the kitchen chaos – after all, I did not create the chaos from choice, but because we are too poor to pay anyone else to do it for us. This was, as usual, a waste of time. He just stayed in the TV room, watching racing.

At about 3 p.m. the man from Bonhams came, and over a brandy we did the paperwork. I asked Arthur to join us but he just told me to deal with it myself. This was the final straw. It seemed to crystallise my certainty that not only do I undertake most of the physical work involved in the shop, but also I shoulder nearly all the responsibilities of our ménage.

I stood, after the 'dogs' had left for the auction rooms in London, looking down the garden and drawing on my third cigarette, finishing my brandy and trying to comfort my sad, self-pitying self. And I realised I should not be sad, that I am lucky to have so much else; all my other dog pictures, my beloved possessions, my blood-relations, my friends, my talents, my health, my Sanka, my cats, my beloved Po Ho – and my Arthur. But I fear my darling Arthur, who has been everything to me for fourteen years, keeps kicking me with his clay feet. He becomes so boorish when he is angry now. He just shouts and bangs doors and feels he has 'won'. I fear that I must now fall back on my own resources and strengths to survive.

I did not marry young because I was always searching for someone stronger, wiser and abler than myself. I thought I had finally found him in Arthur. Gradually – oh so very gradually – I had begun to realise I was wrong; that *I* really was the strong one.

The 'accountant' was a very attractive man indeed, and he had a reputation as a bit of a 'ladies' man'. He had even tried to flirt with my friend Vivian – who christened him 'Fingers' (so it is as Fingers I shall refer to him now). When Arthur took a few days off to get away and play some golf with Shrimp Osborne, it was too much of an opportunity for Fingers to miss, and he made some excuse to his wife and came and spent a night with me at Po Ho. Our affair had reached the stage when this was just a natural progression to romantic heights. It was catastrophic that when Arthur came home, my cleaner, Mrs Bowditch (actually a darling friend and called Mrs Bow-wow by me), in total innocence told him: 'Fingers didn't waste any time after you'd left, he was round here like a shot!'

That was it. Arthur got straight onto the phone to tell Fingers's wife that her husband was having an affair with me. It so happened that I knew Fingers was going to be late home that evening as he had a business meeting in Wincanton. I wanted to warn him that our secret was out and to tell him that he would not get a friendly reception when he got home. I drove off and waited in a lay-by on his route home and stopped his car when it came into sight. I was in a terrible state, but secretly hoping that the crisis would hurry up our divorces. He calmed me down and promised me that

I was not to worry because he would never let me down. He would sort everything out.

Of course, he did not. He calmed his wife down. I calmed Arthur down. The affair continued, but assignations became much more difficult and everything seemed to go wrong for me with Arthur. One night he got so angry with me that he threatened me with a funny old-fashioned revolver gun he had. He said, 'There's two bullets in this. One's for you and the other's for me!' I managed to get to the phone and call 999 and the police car came quickly – with flashing lights alerting the whole village to our little drama. By then Arthur had calmed down and was full of remorse, so all that happened was confiscation of the gun by the police.

Our financial situation had got worse and worse. The shop simply did not generate enough income to meet the mortgage payments and household expenses. We delivered an ultimatum to every household in the village, telling them to use the shop or lose it. The old faithful customers were alarmed at the possibility that the shop might close, but the rest continued to shop in Yeovil or Sherborne.

Once I had banished Arthur into one of the guest bedrooms he naturally was furious and issued his own ultimatum. If we didn't make peace with each other and if I didn't put an end to my affair with Rat (as he had now been named) Arthur would leave me and go and stay with his daughter Sally in London. We had reached crisis point. I had to find out whether Rat's intentions were as honourable as he claimed. He wanted me to get my divorce first, and then he would get his as soon as his late-teenage sons had left school. I had to put him to the test, so I drove to his house near Yeovil. His wife came to the door and I said, 'I have to speak to your husband.' She went to call him, but came back with the words: 'He won't come and speak to you, he's hiding in the greenhouse'!

My world came crashing to the ground. Arthur was leaving me. The house had to be sold – and in spite of his cowardly behaviour when I tried to confront him, Rat continued to pester me and tell me it would all work out when the boys had left school. He still kept saying that he loved me – and, stupidly, I believed him. I was infatuated. In retrospect I am sure that money was the root of all our evils. Rat was an accountant and obviously quite well-off. He had a large, if horrible, modern house and both his boys were at public school. He would have given me security – whereas I dreaded to think what my future would be like, penniless, with Arthur. We simply could not afford to get together again – although, deep in my heart I did still love him and would forever do so. Rat had spoilt everything.

So Po Ho was sold, but not until the beginning of 1979. Over the winter of 1978–79, I rented a former gamekeeper's cottage in wild Dorset countryside close to the village of Rampisham. It was a holiday cottage and fairly sparsely furnished, but I took quite a lot of my own furniture, including my beloved cast-iron bed, which made the cottage really cosy and homely. I also took Sanquhar and the three remaining cats (both corgis had died by then). The animals were in paradise there – they had complete freedom and lots of hunting as well. Sometimes the Cattistock Hunt would come down the track leading to the cottage and beyond, which was a treat to behold.

Sadly, Sanquhar died soon after I left Rampisham, but I was able to bury her in the orchard at Po Ho, next to Morgan, because the house had not yet been sold. I dug her grave myself – and a labrador needs a very deep grave. I managed to get her from the house to the grave in a wheelbarrow, but heaving her out of it and into her grave was impossible. Fortunately my uncle, Pat Waters, called on me at the right moment, and between us we placed her gently in the ground. Before replacing the earth I went round the garden and picked every single rose in bloom and strewed them over her. I then planted an oak tree at her head, as I had done previously for Morgan.

Fingers/Rat was still prowling around and visiting me frequently at Keeper's Cottage. However he would often make arrangements to come to dinner and then simply not turn up. Admittedly he could not contact me because the cottage was without a telephone. Other friends and family were very supportive. In particular, Laurie

Fricker and his girlfriend Annie from Evershot were constant visitors. When a bitter spell of weather arrived, with deep snow and freezing winds, and set in for several days, when all the roads became impassable, they *walked* all the way, tramping a couple of miles through deep snow from Evershot to make sure I was all right. Once the roads became more usable, although the weather was still bitterly cold and snowy, they insisted that I spend a couple of nights with them. I took the animals with me – which was somewhat fraught, as we had to make sure they couldn't escape from the house, which opened out onto the Evershot village street.

One of our old friends in the good old days at Melbury was one John Lake, a bachelor who lived up a narrow lane in the hill above Beaminster. He was a stalwart friend and a huge support to me. His farmhouse was quite grand, and he had noisy peacocks. He would frequently invite me to dinner there with his friends, often including Jim Spicer and his wife – Jim was the MP for West Dorset at the time. I would have been pretty lonely at Rampy had it not been for the kindness of John, my cousins the Pisanis and other friends who helped me through these difficult months.

Chapter Seventeen

When my winter tenancy came to an end and Po Ho had been sold, I had to start looking for somewhere to live. By now I was divorced from Arthur. A divorce that should never have happened; it was something that I was pushed into by Rat. I was very, very unhappy and already questioning the sanity of my behaviour and my brainwashing by Rat. Although I had bought Po Ho and it was in my ownership, I had to give Arthur half the proceeds of the sale, so I had only £22,000 to spend. Meanwhile my cousins Patrick and Mary allowed me to stay in the small cottage that was part of their larger home, Wyndham House, which overlooked Sutton Bingham reservoir and had a beautiful view. The Pisanis stored some of my furniture for me in one of their loose boxes; the rest went into store in Bridport. My life seemed to be in complete limbo. Gradually, however, I began to regain some confidence in myself and to accept the fact that Rat had been cheating on me all the time. I remember his wife saying to me on the disastrous visit to his house when Rat cowered in his greenhouse and refused to confront me, 'I bet he tells you he doesn't sleep with me – well, I can assure you that he certainly does.'

Although all our old friends wished there could be a reconciliation and tried to manoeuvre us back together, that was not to be. Apart from anything else, we simply could not have afforded to start again. By now Arthur was living in London and working for

Paddy, delivering and collecting hire cars. Not a very lucrative job. I still had to find somewhere to live and to earn some money. Some time later, when I had found myself a new home and got myself a job, Arthur was playing golf at Roehampton when he had yet another heart attack. There was some delay while an ambulance was sent for and this time Arthur did not recover. He died on the 8th October 1980. His funeral service in St Clement Dane's Church was a very beautiful and moving one, his coffin borne in with his medals on top of the RAF flag to the magnificent sound of Elgar's music.

My house-hunting strategy had been to study the Ordnance Survey map of the Sherborne, Crewkerne and Ilminster areas and to select villages that looked promising. I then got particulars of cottages in just a few likely villages. One cold Sunday in February 1979, I set off to look at three possible cottages. The first of these was in the village of Hinton St George, near Crewkerne. It was the end property of a terrace of three thatched cottages set at right angles to a lane and approached up a narrow little path. Number 15 was my destination (and, indeed, as it turned out – my destiny). The two cottages I had passed on my way were picture-postcard hamstone buildings and both had pretty gardens, as did Number 15. Mr and Mrs Trinkle, the owners, welcomed me into the hall and through to the kitchen, where a jolly party of friends were having Sunday lunch and evidently enjoying plenty of red wine with it. A small wood-burning stove was glowing in the fireplace, there was pretty Laura Ashley paper on the walls, and I was captivated, completely captivated. I was shown round the rest of the cottage, and it was all exactly what I had hoped to find. As well as the cottage itself, the old wash-house and privy buildings were still in existence. The asking price was £17,500, and I made an offer at that figure at once. I never bothered with a survey – I just *had* to have it. I knew the cats would love it too! By now, sadly, I had no dog.

I did call on two other properties sent to me by the agent – but I told the owners that I had already decided on one in Hinton St George. By April all the formalities had been completed and the cottage was mine and I could arrange to move in.

It is a most unusual cottage in that it's single storey. The terrace had originally been a farmhouse, and my part, the end of the terrace, was thought once to have been either the dairy or a stable. Several alterations and additions had been made since the 1600s, when the farm was thought to have been built. The accommodation now consisted of a quarry-tiled sitting room, with an open fireplace in one corner and with two other doors as well as the entrance door off the hall. One of these doors opened into the main bedroom, the other to a bathroom – which had a bath and basin but no lavatory. To the left of the front door was a room used by the Trinkles as a nursery for their baby (it's now my office). The hallway led into the kitchen, through which one moved on to the 'back-passage' (as I christened it), situated in a horrid Bradstone recent extension containing another bedroom and a cloakroom with lav and wash basin. There was no staircase, although there was some attic space. Under the thatched part of the roof the rafters were simply branches of trees as supports – but they had done their job for nearly four hundred years and showed no signs of giving way.

I made a lot of improvements. My first priority was to break through from the main bedroom into the bathroom, install a lavatory and close up the door from the bathroom to the sitting room. Later on I did up the old wash-house, replaced the mud floor with flagstones and built a wall of cupboards to contain a washing machine and deep freeze. The privy became a garden store. These other works were carried out over a period of several years, but I have ended up with a really cosy and practical but tiny home, which I love.

I moved in to the cottage in April 1979 and began to look for a job. I was fortunate to see an advertisement in the local paper for a secretary to the Sales Manager of the German industrial battery manufacturer Varta. I was first interviewed by the office manager, a lively young woman named Antigone, and then by my prospective boss, Brian Gale, who seemed to approve of me and offered me the job straight away. I started the job soon after my interviews and found myself working with a fantastic crew of fellow workers. We all worked hard, but we also laughed a lot, and the men on the factory floor were always playing tricks on us. As Sales Manager, Brian was frequently away from the office, and he made regular trips to Varta's HQ at Hagen in Germany. This meant I often had a lot of time on my hands, and it was then that I began to write these memoirs. At least I used an electric typewriter then, not a manual – but of course typing was still much harder work than it was when I later had access to a computer.

After about eighteen months Varta decided to move its Industrial Batteries division to their London headquarters; the only part of the operation to remain in Crewkerne was that supplying huge batteries for submarines etc – the rest of us were made redundant. Quite soon I saw an advertisement for a secretary to the chairman of a large building concern in Yeovil – Bartlett Construction Group – whose secretary was about to retire. I was granted an interview with the Personnel Director, Brian Reeves. I sailed through that one and was invited back for a second interview, this time with the chairman himself, Richard Timmis. Also at the interview was his wife, Sue – presumably to satisfy herself that I was not attractive enough or young enough to be a threat. His previous secretary had worked for the company for many, many years, and 'Directors' Reception' really did need smartening up a bit. For instance, my predecessor had always come to work in the same or a similar outfit: a black pinafore over a black jersey, and never any make-up. I was also to work for another director, Ian Crinks, whose office was part of the same suite.

Working with me was a very young, very nice, newly qualified audio-typist. Luckily we were to work together as a good team. Her spelling was pretty awful and so was her vocabulary, but she was really keen to improve, so every day I would make a list of her wrongly spelt words down the left-hand side of a lined A4 sheet, and she would write the words again a few times alongside – she was really grateful for this. She'd also make a note of any words she couldn't understand and next day I would write the meanings alongside. It was very satisfying for me, too, because by the time I moved on to another job she was far more literate as well as being an accurate typist.

At first I was very unhappy in the job. Richard was an extremely demanding boss and he was incredibly hard working. Most of his work was dictated onto a tape recorder – sometimes he would be working so hard that he would dictate while he was in his bath at home – one could hear the water splashing about as he spoke! After a few months I felt I couldn't take any more of his shouting at me one moment and ignoring me the next, so I started looking for another job. Fortunately I was not successful, even though I lied and said I was ten years younger than the truth, because as time went by Richard and I began to get on much better. I learned to understand that the shouting and the ignoring were not meant unkindly, it was just that he was a very brilliant man heading a very successful building and development company, and his mind was totally committed to whatever projects he was involved in at the time.

Having said that, it so happened, after a year or so, I was told that a friend of a friend was looking for an assistant to help her with her expanding public relations business. It was too good an opportunity to miss, so I parted amicably from Richard – little imagining that several years later we'd be working together again. My new boss's largest client was a 3M company and the chief product involved was Scotchgard, a treatment for cleaning and protecting upholstered furniture and carpets. Others were Thinsulate, an insulating fabric for sportswear; a cardboard-based packaging product and an aluminium foil industrial type of insulation fabric – these sound rather boring, but they were not.

My boss was a strikingly attractive woman. Her job was undoubtedly a stressful one and she suffered from ill health. She would then be hospitalised. Somehow her illness did not totally incapacitate her from working, so that every day I would have to visit her in the ward and give her any correspondence that needed input from her. I also had to cover for her in the office and at meetings with clients because, naturally, she did not want her clients to know about her health problems. She was able to compose letters, proposals and press releases from her hospital bed, but I was increasingly taking over more and more of our workload. As soon as she recovered from a 'down' period, she would quickly revert to being the confident and glamorous leading lady of the agency. It became obvious to me that she was beginning to resent the fact that I had been so successful at keeping her clients happy. On one particular occasion, after I'd submitted a draft press release to an important client, the draft was approved without a single alteration and a footnote saying: 'Excellent. Thank you.' My boss was displeased. I suspect that she was anxious that I was getting a bit too close to our clients, and this did not suit her. She had been acting in a less friendly way with me for a couple of weeks, and this was the catalyst. She gave me the sack!

Chapter Eighteen

Mummy, Carol and I had often talked about the possibility of a return visit to India, but in 1983 we decided it was time we did something about it. I was able to negotiate a three-week holiday with Richard to enable such a visit. I think, by then, he was beginning to appreciate me! We did not want to go on any of the existing tours offered in travel magazines; we wanted to plan visits to places that were part of our pasts. Mummy organised our trip brilliantly, helped by Cox & Kings. She told them which hotels we wanted to stay in and the places we wanted to visit. Everything went according to plan. The trip was planned around the places Mummy and Daddy had visited on their honeymoon. Mummy's father had lent them his special coach; one which could be attached to any train. It had a well-furnished living room, bedroom, bathroom and a section reserved for any servants travelling too. They stopped off at Allahabad, Agra, Delhi and on to their destination – the Dal Lake at Srinager in Kashmir.

We took off from Heathrow in our 'Imperial Airways' Trident on the afternoon of Sunday 22nd January 1984. The cloud broke as we were flying over the Alps, then we could see Yugoslavia and Turkey before our first refuelling stop at Kuwait. It was dark by now and we could see hundreds of oil flares burning. Food on board was very tasty, the drinks were free and the stewardess kept us plentifully supplied with baby bottles of whisky, some of which we hoarded against the possibility of deprivation in India.

We arrived at Delhi Airport at 4 a.m. local time after a flight of thirteen and a half hours. A scruffy arrival 'hangar' (it was not much better than that) and tiresome babu officialdom meant long queues, and we felt very tired and a bit irritated. As one was not allowed to change one's money into rupees before arriving in India, we had none for our taxi and had to join a seedy queue at the tatty hut, manned by just one clerk, that called itself The Bank of India. Each transaction took nearly twenty minutes to be dealt with, as every document had to be read, re-read and re-read again. By the time Robin appeared with his wad of rupees we had been nearly two hours on the ground. As soon as we looked ready to leave, porters fought for our baggage, and taxi drivers – all swathed sinisterly in army-type blankets with only their eyes staring out – fought for our custom. All was noise, confusion, hooting of horns, swerving about – and then we were off on the road into the city.

At the airport I saw my first Indian cat. A very smartly marked but rather grubby black and white fellow who was having a great fuss made of him by everyone – but Mummy sternly reminded me that I must not touch any animals in India . . .

The Ashok Hotel was magnificent. A huge sandstone portico with steps leading to a wall of glass doors into a vast hallway of marble, carpeted in red and with groups of red leather sofas set around low marble tables, a fountain playing and masses of flowers. We staggered to our rooms and fell straight to sleep.

Next day we woke to sunshine and warmth. After breakfast we set off to Thomas Cook's offices at the Imperial Hotel to get our rail tickets organised and to check our various reservations. The office was incredible. Straight out of Dickens – all dark brown wood, about eight people crammed into an office about twelve-foot square, desks piled high with pending paperwork and type-writers, telephones and a telex machine that looked as though they'd come out of the Ark.

Once sorted, we strolled down Janpath, which is a very busy, attractive tourist street of lock-up shops, stalls and strolling vendors. Men roasted nuts over little fires, or fried tasty-smelling savoury titbits. Old men swathed in blankets slept on the pavement on charpoys. Mangy but contented-looking pi dogs sniffed about the refuse. The traffic was completely mad. All the cars were Morris Oxfords, either black or white. Discipline was unheard of; they drove on the wrong side of the road, the wrong way round roundabouts if there was no traffic (or even if there was). Quite chaotic – yet they had it down to a fine art.

After tea we managed to contact our new Indian friend, Mr Misra, to whom we had been put in touch by a mutual Indian army friend. He had been unable to meet us at the airport because his driver had been 'indisposed'. He came straight over to the hotel for a drink then took us in his car for a tour of the city. His car was the standard Morris Oxford (black) and he had a lovely old man for a driver. During the drive Mr Misra suddenly stopped the car, said 'I won't be a moment' and went off towards the trees for a pee. We soon got used to the sight of men peeing anywhere they felt like it. Just before the India Gate (the war memorial) we saw a small pavilion; the statue that should have been within conspicuous by its absence. Mr Misra told us, with slight embarrassment, that it used to contain a statue of King George V – so we laughed and made light of it. Mr Misra explained that they had not felt able to replace it with one of their beloved Gandhi, because that person would not have wished to be associated with anything as warlike as a war memorial!

Approaching up the long, wide Rajpath from India Gate we saw the Viceroy's house, now the Presidential Palace or Rashtrapati Bhavan, magnificently illuminated – not with floodlights but with all its features outlined by thousands of fairy lights. We were driven all round the embassy territory, government territory, civil service territory and we were proudly shown the new Drug Research Hospital, with a rather seedy General Hospital on the other side. Alongside were shanties with dentists at work, tethered mules munching and parties round pavement fires. Bright yellow three-wheeler motorcycle taxis

167

nipping in and out – one of these had *ten* people on it – some just hanging on to the shirt tail of the person inside. Humanity seethed. The buses were filled to bursting, people crammed like sardines. On we then went to Delhi Golf Club. Faded Imperial – Mr Misra was very proud of it.

Mr Misra treated the club servants in just the peremptory way the Raj was so criticised for doing – 'Boy! Boy!' Indian whisky is good. Snacks were scrumptious – very hot and highly seasoned.

Just as we got back to the Ashok we overtook a wedding procession approaching the hotel. Groom on a huge white horse that was magnificently attired in brilliant colours and heavily jewelled, as was the groom himself. Attendants waved torches, trumpets blew, we heard our first 'Foo Foo' band and there was singing and dancing and shouting and clapping. The procession wound up the drive to the hotel porch, where Carol and I had stationed ourselves to watch. Rich Indian guests were arriving in their tubby Morris Oxfords, lots of them handsomely turbaned and bewhiskered. Beautiful saried women with gorgeous jewels and children elaborately dressed in frilly Edwardian outfits. We began to feel in a party mood ourselves.

The last time Mummy was in Delhi was in 1937 for the Delhi Horse Show. Daddy's regiment was taking part in the parades and was camped somewhere east of the Rajpath. Her last sight of Lutyens's Viceregal Lodge had been when she entered the main gates to attend a viceregal ball, having dressed for the occasion in an army tent by the light of a hurricane lamp – in a specially grand gown, mail-ordered from England!

Next morning we set off to the Railway Museum, passing Nehru Park and looking at all the Embassy and High Commission buildings. We did see some fascinating rolling stock, but it was all a bit shabby. We saw the Viceroy's coach, the Prince of Wales's coach, a Rajah's coach – and a typical sahib's coach, just as Mummy had so often described these, with comfy living quarters for the sahib and his family and a special compartment marked 'servants' for his entourage! We walked back via the Shantipath, the central avenue with the important embassies down each side. Russian, American, British – each with its own special style of architecture. The Pakistani one was particularly lovely, with three big blue mosaic domes and elaborate iron gates.

After lunch we took a driver and did some sightseeing. First we visited a very old ruined sandstone fort called Ferozshah. Here we saw the first of what were to be armies of the little squirrels that abound in northern India. Mummy suddenly remembered the word for them: 'gilehri' – which impressed our driver no end. We immediately christened them 'Galtieri'. We were surrounded by a little gang of Sikh children, who spoke to us with perfect accents: 'How do you do?' 'It's a lovely day'. This fort is in Old Delhi, which is now completely seedy and a seething mass of overcrowded humanity. There used to be two hotels here that Mummy remembered well: the Swiss House and Maidens. Mummy and Daddy had spent a few nights of their honeymoon at Maidens and we thought we might have tea there. However, when we passed it Mummy was so horrified by its run-down slum-like appearance that she shivered and decided against this. Instead, we proceeded on the first of our three great pilgrimages: my birthplace, Carol's birthplace and our house in Dehra Dun.

The Hindu Rao hospital is on The Ridge, which I described in chapter one. Also on the ridge is the Mutiny Memorial, which I particularly wanted to see. As we reached the steps at the foot of the memorial we noticed a plaque set into the wall that read: 'The "enemy" referred to on this memorial were gallant Indians fighting for our freedom from imperialistic rule'. We climbed the steps to the real memorial and read the names of the officers and men killed and the chronology of the battles on The Ridge. It was a poignant moment.

The Hindu Rao Hospital, where I was born, is now a high-rise slummy hospital. Still being enlarged, there are five- or six-storey buildings with rags hanging out of the windows to dry. Relatives were camped in the grounds and cooking food to take to their sick kindred. All sorts of stalls were selling dirty-looking food, and urns were dispensing tea. Mangy dogs sniffed round scavenging, and the whole atmosphere was thoroughly squalid. At first we could see no sign of the original building – but we persevered. Robin saw it first. A sadly faded crumble of grey stucco. There was the old drive-in porch and a stone stairway leading to a wide verandah with arches, over which moth-eaten rattan blinds hung, mouldy with age. It was not quite deserted; there seemed to be nurses' locker rooms and people drinking tea in murky rooms leading off the verandah. Nobody took the slightest notice of us, so Robin and I had a good snoop round. I met a thin but handsome ginger cat! It was a strange feeling for me to know that over fifty years before I had entered this world in that very place . . .

We drove back through the narrow streets of Old Delhi – traffic completely solid: rickshaws, scooters, three-wheelers, cabs, cows, tongas (horse-drawn carriages), bicycles, bullock carts. Blinding colours and sights – but the smells here were not those of garbage and decay as I'd expected. The overriding smell was that of diesel. We saw a funeral procession – the corpse simply wrapped in a shroud and carried on a stretcher by two bearers – threading its way through the crowds. Our driver told us it was a Mohammedan funeral; the body would be buried, not burned.

Along the Rajpath, stands were being erected for Thursday's Independence Day parade. A hive of activity. Our driver pointed out where the President and Prime Minister would be seated and then 'the seats for very good people – very important people'. Where were we going to be seated, I wondered?

On Wednesday afternoon, we went to Connaught Place. Now a cross between Whitechapel Road and a cowboy town. Mummy told us that in her day it was immaculate, with smart dress shops, hairdressers, jewellers, tearooms etc. The Mayfair of New Delhi. Now it was a shanty town. Pavements were broken up and crumbling. Shops had been divided into tiny kiosks. Lean-to stalls obstructed the arcades. Really rough-looking traders squatted on the pavements selling nuts, vegetables, sticky sweets. Robin was really 'done' by a shoe-shiner who said to him, 'Oh! You have dirty shoes, you have paint on them.' He did. Fresh paint! Obviously just flicked onto him by an accomplice! The man then cleaned his shoes – but removed the inner lining. Robin saw him doing this like a sort of conjuring trick. The rascal said, 'Oh! The nails are showing – they will make holes in your socks. My friend will fix them.' Robin scarpered PDQ!

It was the eve of Independence Day. Everyone was feeling festive, celebrating getting rid of the British. Us. One sensed antipathy. Not quite hostility – just challenging, rather cheeky looks. Our beds were not turned down that night. Our tea tray had not been removed. Perhaps the staff were just overworked; the hotel was full-to-bursting. They did not seem to mind that their city is squalid. That the pavements are disintegrating. That once-elegant buildings have become slums. Even in our five-star international hotel the steps from the garden to the front entrance were slippery with urine. The smell was gasp-making. Within the Ashok Hotel was a haven of cleanliness and peace.

Thursday the 26th January was Independence Day. Mr Misra collected us and we drove to the celebrations. Milling crowds had to be negotiated at high speed over the rough ground and we were terrified of losing each other. Mr Misra strode out so fast, with his dashing scarf streaming out behind him, like Piglet's. We had good seats in the VIP stands, with a splendid view of the saluting base. Mrs Gandhi arrived standing in her open white Jeep to thunderous applause. Then came the President and the King of Bhutan – seated in the British Viceroy's coach with its elegant little parasol.

The parade was fantastic. Splendid marching and bands – every bit as good – if not better – than our own. A twenty-one-gun salute boomed out. Holders of the Victoria Cross and other gallantry awards (*Chakras*) led the rest of the parade. Then guns, tanks, caparisoned camels and colourfully dressed black elephants carrying waving children – the winners of bravery awards for saving their siblings, dogs etc from disasters. We sat surrounded by Russians, one of whom kindly offered me his coat when a cool breeze sprung up. At the end of the parade there was an exciting fly-past – including a 'heliphant' – a helicopter dressed as an elephant, with dangling legs!

Afterwards, Mr Misra came back to the hotel for lunch with us and then Carol, Robin and I went for a saunter through Nehru Park, close to our hotel. This was quite a new park, beautifully landscaped with lots of huge sandstone rocks and bedded out in a very pleasing way with trees, shrubs and plants. We saw three proper family dogs splashing in a pool – two Alsatians and a red setter. Lots of Indian families were strolling about and quietly picnicking.

Next day, in the later afternoon, we set off to see Beating the Retreat. This was not to be the pukka performance but the dress rehearsal. As the Russian Number Two, Mr Ustinov, was to be a guest at the actual performance next day, security was so tight that no tourists were to be allowed. However, it was performed as if it were the real thing and was a fantastic spectacle. Massed bands, pipe bands – all Indian marching music, but all very pleasing to the ears. Camels were stationed motionless on the ramparts, making a spectacular backdrop, and they didn't seem to move for one and a half hours. In the two little 'pagodas' were two cavalry officers on beautiful chestnut horses, holding pennants aloft. The drill was immaculate. Then came splendid sound effects and trumpet echoes to 'Abide With Me' – apparently Gandhi's favourite hymn. Then, suddenly, the illuminations were switched on – the effect was quite lovely.

We were seated among some military families, part of the Signals section controlling the parade. Lots of medals. Officers eating monkey nuts out of paper bags – Indians are potty about monkey nuts! A small child peed as it sat in its seat – no one took the slightest bit of notice. Mummy sat beside a very handsome Sikh major and his family and got into conversation with him. She complimented him on the magnificence of the parade and said it was as good, if not better, than anything she had seen in England! He made a sweeping gesture over the scene with his arm and said, 'Madam, the British gave us all this. Thank you for it!'

On Saturday 28th, we had to make an early start to catch the bus at Connaught Place. Roads were being swept, trash was being collected; comparative cleanliness. One large rat was lying dead on the pavement. One runty puppy was foraging for breakfast. Delhi dogs strolled nonchalantly about. We then took to our bus for a guided tour. First we visited the Jantar Mantar – the stone 'observatory' where you can tell the time, day, month and year by the shadows of the moon and the sun. Then we stopped at a very garish temple called Laxmi Narayan. We saw a woman kissing the feet of a priest and gaudily painted figures of Vishnu and Laxmi, with marigolds strewn at their feet and offerings tossed before them.

We spent a fascinating half-hour at the Nehru Exhibition. There was much ephemera such as his letters home from Harrow and Cambridge, old invitations, old uniforms, wonderful old photographs and many interesting quotations. There was also a representation, done by photographic enlargements, of the cell in which he had been imprisoned and in which he wrote his autobiography. There was a display about Amritsar. I felt the blood of my ancestors pulsing through me.

We were then bussed south to one of the earlier cities of Delhi to see the ruins round the Qutar Mnab, which is a very high, carved sandstone tower, with carved sandstone cloisters arched all round it and lovely gardens. Next we visited the graves of the great – Gandhi and Nehru. After that it was the Jama Masjid – the largest mosque in Old Delhi. It is vast; able to accommodate 25,000 worshippers and covering probably two acres. Outside the mosque was a teeming market through which our bus literally had to fight its way. On the awning above one of the stalls sat a large black and white splodge cat.

Our last visit that day was to Old Delhi itself. It was quite frightening. The seething animal-like crowds. People lying asleep, wrapped shroud-like, on the central reservation of a dual carriageway. Noise. Shouting. Hooting horns. Diesel fumes. Clattering hooves – so much noise, so much activity. It was exhausting. By then we were all very tired, but we managed a visit to the Red Fort before returning to the hotel.

Drinking with Mr Misra in the evening, one of us asked him what he thought of Mountbatten. He told us that if it had not been for Mountbatten he believed that no English family would have left India alive. He thought, possibly quite rightly, that the English had 'set up' Jinnah to provoke partition, and that the English had fanned the flames of the troubles because we could then say 'We told you so!' For some reason, however, the Indians had taken Mountbatten completely to their hearts and felt they could communicate with him and that he would treat them fairly. Mr Misra thought Mountbatten had done 'a wonderful job'.

Mr Misra was extremely worried about our travelling arrangements. He said we were very unwise to be travelling on the trains that we had chosen, and that the 'bedding rolls' that we had ordered would be inadequate and unsatisfactory. He had therefore brought with him a large suitcase containing two very high-class sleeping bags and some warm wool blankets. We took the two sleeping bags, both of which had to be squashed into my large suitcase, and one blanket, but we did not have room for more.

On Sunday morning we were up early again and were driven to Delhi station in the dark. Porters, wearing dirty dhotis and smart rusty-pink cotton jackets, carried our luggage on their heads. We had a large old-fashioned carriage to ourselves on the Taj Express, fully air-conditioned. We had breakfast on the train – delicious vegetable patties, very spicy and hot. On the journey we saw a vast steelworks and a power station, all belching thick black smoke. We saw many small brick works, a concrete factory, lots of light industry. Building work was going on everywhere – always using twig-and-branch string-tied scaffold. Lots of marshalling yards with shunting engines – Delhi seemed to stretch forever. After that is was one vast alluvial plain, intensively cultivated with tiny fields of sugar cane, rape, rice and various other types of grain. At one small village we saw a cane market – hundreds of carts and stacks. We saw bullocks walking round and round in circles at the wells, bringing up the water (and sometimes passing it!). There were lots of water towers too – they were doing a great job on irrigation everywhere. We saw, in the hazy early-morning sunshine, many picturesque scenes of women carrying huge brass water-pots on their heads, their saris billowing gently in the breeze.

The little villages consisted of thatched mud huts, barely high enough in which to stand up. Animals were tethered close – bullocks, cows with their calves, cows being milked, dogs, pigs, chickens. Huddled squatting bodies were breakfasting in the open round little fires. Everywhere there was frantic brushing of teeth. A few children were bathing in a water-spout, bullock-carts ambled along dusty tracks, sandy red, from village to village. Not a car to be seen.

We were much aware of military activity. Several very long troop trains were loaded with tanks, all covered with lashed-down canvasses. These were extended at the ends to form tent-like structures in which the soldiers in charge sheltered. There were many cantonments, all very active and with much evidence of spit-and-polish and white paint. Electrification work was taking place all along the line, the cause of many hold-ups to the Taj Express. We saw many freight trains – all freight seemed to travel by train in India.

Mathura, between Delhi and Agra, is a big railway junction. Here, the lines from Calcutta and Bombay converge on their approach to Delhi. Mummy had memories of travelling from Agra to Delhi on stage three of her honeymoon and arriving at Mathura to encounter one of their friends standing on the platform, his bearer beside him carrying a tray with a bottle and three glasses upon it! The friend joined them on the train and they sipped champagne all the way to Delhi!

Mummy also told us a story about her grandfather – a very naughty small boy. He had been travelling on a train and was fascinated by the lavatory arrangements, just a hole in the floor. He thought he'd do a little experiment and dropped his puppy down through the hole onto the rails while the train was moving. He was given a thrashing when his action was discovered.

The Taj Express was anything but an express. It crawled along most of the way, and top speed was about 50 mph. At the numerous halts in the middle of nowhere, people got down from the train and strolled up and down the line to see what was going on. This is apparently routine. The engine driver would always give a hoot a minute or so before he actually set off again, so that people could clamber back on board.

We were met at Agra Cantonment station by the Thomas Cook representative from Taj Travel, who was very helpful. He got us into a taxi and assisted us when we reached the Clarks Shiraz Hotel. This was a ten- to fifteen-year-old building on the site of the orig- inal Clarks Hotel at which Mummy and Daddy had spent part of their honeymoon. It had a peaceful and well-tended garden full of colourful flowers, and we spent a restful afternoon recovering from the journey – the train had arrived three hours late! I had a terrible fright when I was bitten by a 'Galtieri' who nipped my finger, thinking I was offering him food. May God protect me from rabies!

Before sunset we went to visit the Taj Mahal, of which we had a distant view from our bedroom window. It really was as beau- tiful as we'd heard – and whiter than we expected. We sat in the gardens, waiting for the sun to go down and seeing the colour grad- ually changing from white to creamy pink to rosy red.

Next day our early-morning-tea (*chota hazri*) bearer was a Christian called Jacob, who had been in the Dogra Regiment. Mummy had a long chat with him. After three days much of her Hindustani had come back to her, and they spoke to each other in a mixture of that and English. He said: 'Those who remember the British have great affection for them.'

We went next morning for a second visit to the Taj Mahal. At first it was quiet there, but the crowds soon built up and milled noisily about. The hubbub in the sacred tomb was awful. People were shouting to make echoes; people were calling for *baksheesh* (a tip). Horrid. The river looked lovely; the water was very low and there were wide, wide sandbanks, with buffalo wallowing, a few dogs bathing and playing, and dhobis at work with their washing spread out to dry. After that it was Agra Fort. A beautiful building, but, like everything else, it looked uncared for. We also visited the 'Baby Taj', on the other side of the river. It was very pretty and there were no tourists there (except us) to spoil it.

After lunch at the hotel, we were off to the abandoned village of Fatehpur Sikri. The drive was quite interesting; through the narrow slum streets of Agra, past alleys where our driver said untouchables lived – 'very dirty people', he said! Our driver stopped to buy some Paan (a mouth freshener and drug), and I watched the boy sitting cross-legged 'butter' a thin green leaf, fold it and hand it over. We then passed cloth shops, leather shops, barbers, cobblers, jewellers, spice shops, ironmongers. We even passed a large emporium with 'By Appointment to Queen Mary' painted upon it in large scarlet letters. Then it was the suburbs and villages, where potters were at work turning their wheels manually with long sticks, getting up speed and then shaping their pots. Out into the countryside we saw many, many birds – even some hovering vultures. The mud huts here were really cosy looking – nicely shaped with little curved staircases, all made of mud, and with neatly thatched roofs.

We really enjoyed Fatehpur Sikri, as there were only a few people there and it seemed well cared for. At the height of its glory it had been larger than contemporary London!

Next day, Tuesday 31st, was another hot and sunny one and I took myself for a stroll around to look at the ruins of British bungalows. The garden walls were broken and falling down, tops of gateposts had fallen to the ground, gates were either missing, off their hinges or bent and rusty. Gardens had reverted to scrub with grazing goats, chickens and squatting humanity. I was pestered by rickshaw men and children – but the children are quite adorable and say, 'Allo', 'You English?', 'Very nice day' and love to talk and giggle. Several old men said, 'Good morning Memsahib'. I had a long perambulatory chat with a nice old rickshaw wallah. He told me he had been in the army under the British and was pleased when I told him my father had been a soldier in India too. He pointed out that all the slummy bungalows had been 'very good houses when the British here. Very good gardens then'. He said of the ruins of a large house on a nearby hill that it had been the house of a 'very good, very rich British sahib'. When I eventually managed to get away from him and said, politely; '*Chella jaow*' he laughed like mad and said, 'Very good Hindi!'

I had enjoyed Agra very much and was sad to say goodbye to it that morning. Our nice Taj Travel man turned up in a huge blue American limousine to take us to the airport. He said he had bought it second hand from a diplomat 'very cheap'. We arrived in Lucknow at teatime after a comfortable flight in a twin-engined Avro, which Robin said later must have been over thirty years old. There was the usual hassle over tipping the porter boys, who, in spite of notices in the arrival lounge indicating that the charge is one rupee per bag, demand eight rupees for four bags because two boys carry them!

The Carlton Hotel in Lucknow was Indo-Imperial supreme. A two-storey 'bungalow' in style with verandahs all around each floor onto which all the rooms open – no corridors. The building is in the rust-ochre the Indians love so much and which I had begun to find pleasing myself. Reception was pure Somerset Maugham. Dark mahogany desk, primitive switchboard, dark panelling, a huge stuffed tiger in a glass case (shot in 1962 by a Mr Singh). All the brass was bright, our welcome was warm, and all augured well.

Shock hit us when our boy let us into our rooms. We entered a cavernous sitting room with shabbily carpeted cement floor, a divan, two plastic-covered chairs (the divan was a low one, for squatting on), a wooden office-type desk, an archaic telephone with all the wires worn to the metal and fluorescent strip lighting. This room led to a windowless bedroom with two charpoys and a school-type bedside table with a rickety old anglepoise lamp on it. Behind this was a little dressing room which led into the bathroom. This bath-room would have to be seen to be believed – even my photos could not do it justice. A *vast* ancient bath with the enamel chipping off, one chrome tap and one brass tap of entirely different vintage and a plug on a piece of slimy string. A rather elegant Edwardian hand basin with spaghetti-like pipes weaving over the wall, and a filthy brown-stained lav with a pull-the-plug cistern ten feet above it on the wall. Mummy remembered bathrooms like this when they had un-plugged-in baths and a commode that had to be emptied by a sweeper (an untouchable). When we investigated the rear of the building we could see the old steps leading up to what used to be the outside entrance and is now walled up. One left this door open after one had relieved oneself, as a tactful sign to the sweeper that his services were required to remove the 'spoil'. In fact, our present bathroom was luxurious in comparison to that.

Carol and Robin's room was worse than ours – it did not even have carpet on the floor. We had to laugh at our plight, and in an odd sort of way it put us into a great mood. After all, this was *really* seeing India.

We had tea on the lawn and enjoyed, again, a beautifully cared-for garden. Later we visited the Simba Bar and treated ourselves to proper drinks again. Pictures of fierce tigers, panthers and chee-tahs surrounded us. In the dining room was a stuffed leopard. We had an excellent dinner and were in very good spirits. There was a pleasant atmosphere here, and in spite of the lack of 'facilities' we felt very much at home and fully able to face our awesome sleeping quarters. It was all very 'native' and much more exciting.

On Wednesday the 1st February, cough, hawk, spit and the clatter of the 'boys' on the verandah woke us this morning. This was accompanied by the chatter of parakeets, which sweetened the sound.

The electric wiring in this hotel was quite amazing. Worn-to-the-wire flexes of the old-fashioned fabric-covered variety snaked all over the floor. These flexes were all much longer than necessary and were full of knots. The wonky anglepoise in Robin and Carol's room did not even have a plug on the end. The strength of the incoming power seemed to vary, which made the lights flicker and dim all the time, and every now and then go out altogether.

Our suite was scented with Indian Izal; softly in the sitting room and bedroom, powerfully in the bathroom. The management had thought of everything – there was even a pack of lavatory fresh-ener stuck on our bedroom wall.

After breakfast we tried to phone Mr Misra's cousin, Doctor Shukla. We tried again and again – but always 'the switchboard is out of order'. Luckily, Dr Shukla was expecting us and eventually he called us. Robin managed to get someone to go down to the station and do the dirty work of organising the booking of our sleepers and bedding rolls. So far, so good. Dr Shukla and his two sons, Ashok and Prashad, arrived about 6.30 p.m. and we had drinks. Dr Shukla said he would take us to the Chutter Munzl tomorrow. Everything had been arranged. He said that in the afternoon his sons would take us sightseeing. Our little party was going well and we were just waiting for a further supply of drinks when Mrs Shukla and a friend arrived. The friend had fallen out of a rickshaw the previous day and had his arm in plaster. It was a 'dry day' today – they have these on the 1st and 7th of each month, because these are pay days, to prevent the populace from spending their wages on alcohol. Mrs Shukla explained that it was because Gandhi disap-proved of alcohol that the 'dry days' came about. 'He would have preferred us to drink something different!' she said – which we thought was rather daring of her, as she was a Hindu and wore a caste mark on her forehead. She was, however, very emancipated and had a high-powered job in an advertising agency. Her friend turned out to be her boss. He was head of a large agency with branches all over India. Our party had been a great success.

At dinner that night we had the same nice elderly waiter. Mummy began talking to him and he told us he had been a soldier in the Poona Horse. Mummy told him that she had a cousin who had been in that regiment, John Wakefield. The old boy's eyes lit up with delight and he *beamed* with joy. 'He was *my* officer!' he said. He reeled off the names of others he'd known in the regiment – and he even knew the names of the girls they'd married! He was going to write a letter and give it to us tomorrow evening for Mummy to deliver to John Wakefield. 'He will not have forgotten me,' he said. 'He will remember Lala!'

Two cats, both a sort of mangy grey colour with brown spots, sported themselves along the upstairs verandah that afternoon, playing aggressive games and occasionally having a vicious fight!

On Thursday 2nd February Lucknow promised to be the high spot of our trip. We had a fantastic time that day. Dr Shukla and Ashok called for us at twelve and took us to the Chutter Munzl Palace, by now the Indian Drug Research Institute. We were first taken to the director's office and Dr Shukla explained that we were on a sentimental journey and wanted to see anything that still remained of the old Chutter Munzl Club. The director was proud of his institute and wanted to show us *everything* – including the animal house. He was most disappointed when we said we did not want to go near any of the animals. 'You do not like animals?' 'Yes, we *do* like animals!' I said. Dr Shukla then explained that we did not wish to see the animals used for experiments – to which our guide replied: 'We do not butcher animals, we do experiments on animals for the benefit of mankind.'

The front of the building and the gardens were little changed. The porch was draped in bougainvillea, the sweeping lawns, the pots for plants, the statues 'all the same' said Mummy. Inside the building, the rooms had all been partitioned off into boxy offices. We saw laboratory staff carrying trays of things in bottles – the bottles all looked filthy and there was not a white coat to be seen. The old swimming pool, a white marble pool with black and white chequerboard marble round it, is now used as a ping-pong room. It had a sort of mezzanine floor erected over it, on which were the tables of the staff canteen.

Our guide was quite moved to be told, when he showed us the old ballroom, that this was the very place where our mother and father had first met. Mummy said the room was definitely recognisable – the stage where the band used to play still had the white Mogul arch over it but the old wooden floor – once beautifully sprung and said to be the finest dance floor in India – had been concreted over. The elegant pillars that used to run down each side, separating the dancers from the sitters-out, had by then been boxed in with plywood 'to make it more modern'! We were shown the tunnels beneath the palace, which Mummy had not known existed, that run for nearly a mile to The Residency (the official headquarters at the centre of the British area of government of the city) and were very useful at the time of the Siege in 1857.

In the afternoon we sat in the hotel gardens. There was no sign of Ashok to take us sightseeing. Perhaps we had misunderstood? We watched one of yesterday's cats – he was obviously suffering from wounds sustained in the previous day's battle, as he was limping along the ramparts on three legs, holding the fourth self-consciously aloft. Robin, Carol and I went for a walk to the Botanical Gardens at Sikandar Bagh – planted to cover the site of the pitched battle of November 1857. The gardens covered over an acre and were full of roses, dahlias, gladioli, canna lilies, sweet peas, cacti, masses of different varieties of trees, herbaceous borders and fresh green lawns. We also visited a rather tatty tomb, Shah Najaf Imambara. This, too, had been the scene of desperate fighting during the second and successful relief of the Siege of Lucknow.

The evening brought a slight drizzly rain and thunder and lightning. At seven, Dr Shukla called for us to take us for drinks at his brother's house. It was an old house, with pillars, tucked behind a modern block of flats. There was a slight hiatus soon after we arrived, as the electricity supply suddenly failed for the second time that day. Eventually we were all settled and given whisky and tasty snacks, including some small canapés of baked beans on toast! Dr Shukla II was a highly educated man. He had been to Oxford and obtained a doctorate of Philosophy. He had then joined the Indian Civil Service and was for ten years in London at the Indian High Commission. He loved England and all things English and he had sent his daughter to school there. The British things he liked best were whisky, fried plaice and chips, Brussels sprouts and Marmite! He had an Indian servant. A young lad. 'He is training,' Dr Shukla said. Our host had his leg in plaster of Paris as a result of an accident. 'My driver had a very good chicken curry for lunch and he fell asleep at the wheel!' he explained. The room was furnished in

English country-house style, with chintz curtains and linen-covered sofas and chairs with plumped silk cushions. Dr Shukla II had a remarkable voice; perfect English, of course, but with a very old-fashioned way of speaking. He was delightful company and it was difficult to tear ourselves away.

Dr Shukla I took us back to the hotel, where we had yet another delicious curry, and our friend, Lala of the Poona Horse, gave Mummy his letter for posting to John Wakefield.

Next day Dr Shukla collected us for our promised tour. He took us first to see the Martiniere, a staging post for the refugees at last leaving the city after the Siege, and then to the nearby Dilkusha. The Martiniere became a boys' public school ('Kim' went there) after the Mutiny had been settled and the Dilkusha reverted to being a palace with pleasure gardens. After this we went to visit 2 Bandariah Bagh, the house where my Aunt Pamela had been born and where she and Mummy lived for several years while their father, our Buddha, was General Manager of the East Indian Railway and based in Lucknow. 'Bandariah Bagh' means 'the road of the monkeys'! The garden used to have a tennis court, lawns and flowerbeds. It was now overgrown and neglected, and the house looked poorly maintained, but not filthy. A modern 'cottage' had been built by the entrance gate. Mummy rang the doorbell and introduced herself to the present owner, a charming Indian woman with two small children, who invited us in for tea. She was very interested to hear that Mummy had lived in her house all those years ago.

Our final call that day was to The Residency. It was an emotional visit to see this beautiful building, half ruined and pockmarked with shell shots. Happily, all the ruined buildings were obviously now well cared for. Dr Shukla told us that all the ruins were floodlit at night – he could see them from his office. Although the buildings were ruins, and none of them had roofs, their skeletons were reasonably intact. Some of the fireplaces were still there and quite a lot of the ornamental plasterwork too – which was amazing after 130 years. All the buildings were constructed with tiny hand-made bricks, plastered over. Most of the plaster had gone by then, so the general effect was a lovely soft, rosy red. We returned to the Carlton Hotel, and Dr Shukla had tea with us before we all exchanged addresses and bade him fond and grateful farewells.

Next morning we had to make an early start for the next stage of our pilgrimage. As we might have expected, our driver, Mr Khaki, did not turn up at 6.10 a.m. as arranged and we had to find another. Lucknow Station is like a palace, red sandstone and white, with towers, minarets and porticos. The interior was vast and, for India, pretty clean. We had been expecting the worst, after Mr Misra's warning, so we were pleasantly surprised by both our sleeping compartment and our bedding rolls – which had lovely clean scarlet wool blankets. We played a game of bridge and scoffed the delicious packed supper the hotel had provided for us. Then we tucked ourselves up for the night and slept well.

I woke with a start when Mummy suddenly said, 'My God! It's eight o'clock!' which was the time we were due to arrive at Dehra Dun. In fact it was only 7 a.m. but we dressed quickly thinking we would soon be there. However, we crawled along for another hour and a half – still, apparently, down in the flat Ganges plain. Eventually another passenger told us that we had not even reached Hardwar and were over five hours late due to fog in the night. We reached Hardwar at noon. Just as Mummy had prophesied, there were monkeys everywhere. They came along the railings beside the carriages looking for food. One had a yellow plastic carrier bag full of delectables and sat picking out morsels, examining them carefully, then either eating them greedily or throwing them down onto the track.

Drawing out of Hardwar we caught glimpses of the Ganges, then we plunged into deep cuttings, a couple of tunnels and out into the jungle and the foothills of the Shiwalik Mountains. Quite soon, Mummy said; 'This is the Doon!' and after crossing another wide riverbed we approached the outskirts of Dehra Dun. The station, although very crowded, was extremely organised and very clean. It was 1 p.m. – we were only five hours behind schedule.

An excellent driver took us the hour's journey up to Mussoorie.

An unbelievable road of intricate hairpin bends and spectacular views of the hill station spread out high, high, high above us; 6,000 feet above us. Snow had fallen in Mussoorie – not much, but it lay in shaded pockets on the road, and the hillsides were sprinkled with white. We were quite cold when we alighted, as the sun was by then off the front of the Savoy Hotel. 'Reception' was in a sort of Swiss cottage with a verandah and much ornamental woodwork. Inside, the carved wood counter was exactly as it must have been built, eighty-five years before. A small wood fire was burning in a rather primitive grate, and all the old brass notices – VISITORS, MAIL, RECEPTION etc – were in lovely ornate lettering, well worn, and obviously original. Our hearts began to sink as we went on a route march towards our quarters in what Mummy said used to house the 'Bachelors' Wing', up stone steps, along a verandah and into the icy-cold and sparsely furnished rooms. Our 'boy' took us to see the dining room, which was miles away and up numerous flights of steps. By the time we got there, Mummy was in a state of collapse and could hardly breathe. We panicked a bit and were unanimous that we could not stay in this horrible place a moment longer! I went off back to Reception to try to telephone to our contacts for their advice.

Jim Keelan, Mummy's half-uncle who lived in Mussoorie, turned out not to be on the telephone. Princess Sita of Kapurthala (she and her late husband had been good friends of Mummy's father) was away from home, and there was still no reply from Khamal Prasad, Mr Misra's nephew, whom we had tried unsuccessfully to reach on the phone earlier from Dehra Dun. I explained to the dear little man on reception duty that my mother could not stay up here for more than one night, and he quite understood this. It was, of course, the altitude that was having this effect on her. We were 7,000 feet up. He set about organising fires for our rooms, extra blankets for the beds and generally making an enormous fuss of us. Electric fires were brought to supplement the wood, and everything began to take on a rosier hue. A very reasonable dinner was served in our room, hot-water bottles were put in our beds and we began to feel quite cosy and settled. There was no plug on the end of the flex from our bedside light, and as Mummy needed a light to read by when she woke up in the night, I had to take the plug from the fire and join it to the wires of the bedside light, but I could not get the light to work. In the morning I found out why. There was another splendid Indian connection halfway along the flex, with the two wires roughly tied together – one join had come apart – no insulating tape or anything like that! When we got into bed, Mummy had another attack of 'the altitudes' and could hardly breathe, which was very alarming. I do not know what I would have done had we needed a doctor in the night. Fortunately the attack did not last long and she actually slept well.

In the morning I opened the sweeper's door to our bathroom and there before me was the blinding sight of the sun shining upon range upon range of ever-higher mountains, and on the horizon the scintillating white of the everlasting snows on the Himalayan peaks. I had to stand enthralled for several minutes in the bitter cold – for there was snow in the yard below the crumbling wood-work of the balcony outside. I say it was crumbling – it was worse than that. It was a death trap. Parts of it had completely rotted away and there were just gaping holes through to the yard below.

Mummy and I had breakfast in bed and then we held a conference. After consulting Mummy's eight-inch-to-the-mile map of Mussoorie, on which were the names of all the houses – Lilac Cottage, The Nook, Rose Cottage, Kincraig, Mon Repos etc we decided it would be too far and too slippery with snow to walk round to Jim Keelan's house and make contact that way. Instead, Carol and I set off to walk round 'The Camel's Back'. The views in every direction were breathtaking. To the south we could see the road snaking and writhing its way like vermicelli down to Dehra, with a background of range upon range of hills, with the Doon shrouded in mist. We went to the English cemetery, which is terraced in a pine wood, facing the distant snowy peaks. Although the cemetery was probably not officially tended, it was not in bad condition. The paths were quite discernable and the flights of steps were not too overgrown. On one outcrop, bullocks were grazing and an Indian family occupied a small bothy, but there were no obvious signs of human bones sticking out of a collapsing hillside, as we had been warned there might be!

By the time we returned to the Savoy, a regal luncheon table had been set up in the courtyard. In surrealist splendour it awaited us. Four straight-backed chairs were set round a white-robed square table. A good lunch was proudly served by two ancient *khitmugars* wearing soiled and shabby maroon coats and caps; each man exquisitely drilled. Plates were meticulously dusted over before being placed precisely on the table, with the words 'Savoy Hotel' carefully positioned at exactly 'noon'.

The sun shone and we were lovely and warm. It was really too early for flowers to be in bloom, but wisteria, jasmine, climbing roses and honeysuckle twined up the wooden pillars and balconies of the verandah. One could easily visualise, now that one had seen this place, the nostalgia of people who remember the life that was lived here in the old days. The morning strolls along The Mall to change one's books in the library, the band playing on the bandstand, meetings for coffee, walks in the pine woods, tennis and riding and picnics. Tea in the Palm Court with an orchestra or a piano playing. *Chota pegs* before dinner with friends. Dances in the vast ballroom.

Earlier in the morning the manager, Mr Maduban, had taken us all round the hotel and told us the history of how it came to be built. There had been some sort of great drama – he could not remember the details – of a jealous squabble in which someone was shot dead! He told us with great pride as he guided us round that everything was 'still the original'. It certainly was. Even the furniture was the original – about 1880-ish. Huge brass pots held ferns and aspidistras. English sporting prints adorned the walls. Mahogany and green baize gloomed the Billiard Room. Vast Victorian wardrobes graced the bedrooms. It was a complete museum. It would be the perfect setting for a film of the sahibs and memsahibs at play!

For me, in spite of the spartan accommodation, Mussoorie was the highlight of our stay in India and really evoked the past of my Keelan and Dillon forebears. I could visualise the ghost of my great-grandfather sitting, just as Mummy had described, beneath the 350-year old Deodar tree under his sunshade, wearing a panama, enjoying his favourite view and escaping the sun, of which he had a horror. He had been a High Court judge in Allahabad, and used to spend the whole of the summer in Mussoorie.

It was very sad to have to leave Mussoorie. Our driver took us carefully down the hill. He managed to persuade the Gurkha guard to allow us into the Dehra Dun cantonment. He had been in the army himself; he knew 4 Ghangora, our first bungalow, and was able to take us there – but he chickened out of taking us as far as 7 Ghangora, our second bungalow, as he lost his nerve and didn't dare go any further. Our driver also knew where to find the Coronation Hospital – passing on the way the Dehra Dun Club, which Mummy recognised straight away. The hospital was in much better condition than poor Hindu Rao's house and Mummy was easily able to point out the window of the room in which Carol had been born. Dusk was falling fast by now, but Robin managed to take the ritual photograph of mother and child at the site of the confinement.

We had a couple of hours to wait for the overnight train to Delhi, so we installed ourselves in the very spacious first class waiting room. We soon got chatting to a man who had just dropped his twelve-year-old son off at his boarding school – a special school for deaf boys. He was a much-travelled man, who had qualified as a metallurgist at Manchester University, worked for six years in Norway, knew Germany and Italy well and spoke several languages as well as perfect English. Our party was then joined by a Gunner Major, also travelling on our train. He was dressed in a tweed jacket, grey flannels and sober tie. The Indian military are *so* English.

Although we left Dehra Dun half an hour late, we arrived on schedule in Delhi at 7 a.m. having had a very comfortable night and been revived by hot, sweet *chai* somewhere along the line. The streets as we drove to the Ashok Hotel were empty and tidied up. It was a lovely dawn, and returning to Delhi was almost like coming home.

On several occasions, when we were lunching in the Samovar restaurant at the hotel, we had seen a party of obvious film people lunching there too, one of whom had a very familiar face. It turned out to be Edward Woodward. We had not expected Mr Misra to appear that evening (we thought he must have had enough of us by now), but at 7 p.m. there was a knock at the door and there he was. He came in and had a drink – and another and another. Mr Misra kindly insisted that he was taking us out 'to eat real Indian food' – and we did not need much persuasion before accepting. When we had piled into his car he said, 'First I think I will take you to meet one of our great warriors of the Indian Army, an old friend of mine, General Candeth.' Out to the suburb of Kailash we drove. We turned off the main road, turned again, and went down a quiet avenue of houses until we reached the general's house. A fine white building, three storeys high and brightly lit.

Mr Misra knocked at the door and suddenly – could we believe our ears? A more-English-than-the-English Poona voice: 'Do come *in*. What a nice surprise!' We were ushered into a room too British Colonial to be true. Large and lofty, with an enormous tiger skin with a mounted snarling head on one wall, a cheetah on another, a Siberian seal on a third and skins of various exotic prey scattered on the furniture. Good rugs. A vast white sofa, comfortable armchairs and a table with decanters and bottles of mixers. At the far end of the room was General Candeth's dining area, again well furnished and with a fine oak dresser with a collection of good china displayed on it. The table was set for the general's dinner: knives, forks, spoons, wine glass, napkin, bowl of fruit, tray of chutneys etc.

Once we were settled with our drinks, the general and Mummy got talking and discovered that they had numerous mutual friends and acquaintances in common. The general insisted that Mummy should return the following January for the Regimental Reunion. This would be the fiftieth anniversary of the formation of an Indian regiment that Daddy had helped to organise. Mummy protested that she was too old – but neither man would take no for an answer.

The general must have been seventy, but he looked much younger. He was very smartly dressed in grey flannels and a tweed jacket. He was a 'perfect English gentleman', with white hair and moustache and perfect manners. A very interesting and lively man. Mr Misra had told us that he had reached the very top of the army. He had been in charge of the campaign to annexe Goa from the Portuguese and of battles in the Punjab war. He had been highly decorated for valour.

We were shown his collection of military swords, including some beautiful jewelled *kukris* and a sword of the Nagas from the Burma border, used for human sacrifices. In his study, he also had a Snaffles picture of a mountain gun team and many interesting pictures and relics of his distinguished career. He had a signed photograph of Prince Philip, given to him because he was head of the Duke of Edinburgh Award Scheme in India.

The Siberian seal, he told us, is an extremely rare animal. It is a freshwater seal, only found in the wildest lakes of Siberia. He had been extremely privileged to be invited by the Russians, at the end of a visit to Moscow to buy tanks, to go on *shikar* (a shooting trip) to this wild area, where foreigners are not normally allowed.

Not until 10 p.m. did we tear ourselves away, taking the general with us to the Moti Mahal restaurant in Kailash. A dimly-lit room with khaki-coloured tablecloths and napkins and very wide black leather seats with leather bolsters at the back, for squatting on. We had a delicious dinner and Mr Misra and General Candeth accompanied us back to the Ashok. It was midnight before we hit the sack.

On our last afternoon we did some shopping, had tea in the garden of the Imperial Hotel, where a small black cat came and joined us, and began to face the fact that in the small hours of tomorrow morning we had to leave this incredible country – in which we were feeling more and more at home as each day passed. My feelings about the people and the place had changed a lot since we first arrived, and instead of feeling a stranger and an outsider I felt, more and more, as if I belonged here and that part of me was going to stay behind and beckon me back again.

All the same, I was pleased to be back in England and on my way home to my cottage in glorious Somerset.

Chapter Nineteen

I had by now managed to wean myself from Rat and was a completely free spirit, but I hated being on my own and I made sure that most evenings and weekends were spent with my relations or friends. I was very fortunate in having a lot of both. My beloved aunt and uncle, Mary and Lionel Carey, now lived in Sherborne, and Tuesday evenings were always spent with them with spirited conversation, reminiscences and plenty of Grouse. Another evening each week I'd spend with my other aunt and uncle, Pam and Jimmy James, who by then had moved to Ilminster. Their daughter Victoria (my god-daughter) and her husband also lived nearby, so I spent some evenings with them. Importantly, too, I saw lots of Patrick and Mary Pisani, who had been so good to me when I was in the depths of misery and who had so kindly lent me their cottage after my tenancy of Keeper's Cottage came to an end.

By this time, Vivian was also on her own. There had been unhappy dramatic events in her life as well as mine. She knew that Daniel fancied one of her best friends and she had begun to suspect that a relationship was developing between them. Once a week Daniel and his 'lady friend' would go to French lessons in Sherborne. Vivian's suspicions became so strong that she decided to set a trap. She (very cleverly I thought) fixed up a tape recorder in Daniel's van and set it to run just before he left home (The Nook in Melbury, which they were by then renting from my Aunt Lirlie) for his French lesson. The tape duly produced evidence of conversation and activity enough for her to have more than necessary to support her action for a divorce – which she had actually already been contemplating because the marriage was no longer a happy one.

So, Vivian and I were two 'girls' on the loose, determined to have fun. Once a week we'd go and have supper in The Rose and Crown in Dinnington, on part of the old Fosse Way a mile away from Hinton St George. The pub was known by its regulars as 'The Docks' because a fantasy had grown up around it that there was a railway line with a level crossing just outside the entrance and also a dockyard. Spoof photos illustrating these conveniences hung on the old tobacco-stained walls of the pub. It was lovely, silly fun. The landlord, John, was a great character, and his wife, Wendy, was a gem of a cook in the kitchen, producing delicious meals for which she charged very little. I suppose the customers, mostly ancient old men, were a bit wary of women, especially unaccompanied women, and at first we were viewed with deep suspicion, meaningful looks and heavy silences. Gradually the ice melted and we began to be treated as friends. Usually when we arrived at the bar a cry would go up; 'Hooray! Here come the ladies.' Every Christmas Eve the pub held a carol service; someone played on the ancient upright piano, mugs and glasses were always kept full and everyone joined in the singing with gusto. Lessons were read by local 'celebrities', such as Paddy Ashdown (who lived in a nearby village) and Peter Longhurst (the first Brit to qualify for a journey into space, but who never got the chance to take off). David Broadbent, 'Broadbean', performed as compère, and it was all very jolly. When I first went to live in Hinton, David was my next-door neighbour, so I knew him well.

In a previous chapter I wrote about the annual 'White Brothers' crazy cricket matches. After the death of Robert White, the venue for these had moved to the sports field in Melbury Osmond. They were great occasions; those fielding took their pints out onto the pitch with them and there was always a large crowd of spectators to cheer and boo the umpire's decisions. At the match held in July

1985, an event occurred which was to change my life completely and unexpectedly. Vivian had invited me to join her and one of her girlfriends to watch the match. It was a hot, hot afternoon and we consumed plenty of wine as we sat on the grass and spectated. I had spotted a very beautiful vintage Lagonda parked alongside the other cars and said how much I admired it. Vivian and Daniel, still together at this point, were into vintage cars; Daniel owned a chain-driven GN and he was also allowed to exercise Lord Stratcona's vintage Mercedes. Vivian replied that the Lagonda belonged to one of their friends, Martin Holloway, and she said, 'You must meet him. He's also got a vintage aeroplane, and I know you like aeroplanes.' So we were introduced, and Vivian told Martin that she knew I would love to have a flight in his Stampe bi-plane. He said of course he would take me up and I gave him my phone number. It was not for another month until the weather and my diary made the flight possible.

Martin had been very persistent in trying to get me my flight in the Stampe – but eventually I was free to accept his kind invitation and I looked forward to my long-awaited treat.

Before I left Bartletts for the PR company I had met, through my job, a character called Barry Tanner. He was a tenant of Richard's on an industrial estate in Chard, where he ran a small woodworking business. During the negotiating of his lease, he made several visits to our office and I got talking to him and found him both attractive and interesting, with a rather mad sense of humour. He was 'into' carthorses and old agricultural machinery, and I was interested too. Of course he eventually asked me out to dinner and a new friendship slowly developed between us. He was a complete extrovert. All my family and friends seemed to like him and I came more and more to enjoy his company. I'd known him for only about three months when the day arrived for my flight in Martin's plane. I was very excited, and Barry wished me luck.

The great day finally came on the 30th August 1985. Daniel and Vivian drove me down to Chalmington Manor, near Cattistock, where the Stampe was kept on a grass strip belonging to a gentleman called Brian Woodford, to meet Martin and be introduced to the most beautiful creature I had ever seen: Martin's bright-red Stampe. I was duly strapped in, photographs were taken – and then we were off. We flew down to Bridport, then along the coast over Golden Cap to Lyme Regis and up the old railway line to Axminster, Sutton Bingham, Melbury and then back to the strip. It had been heavenly.

That flight was the first of many to which Martin treated me that late summer. They were not the only treats – he started taking me out to dinner and to fly-ins around the country where I met many fellow Stampe owners and saw other interesting aircraft. Not only was I up in the air in the Stampe, but also, as Martin was virtually Brian Woodford's chief pilot, I flew in all his other aircraft too – including the de Havilland Gipsy Moth, Tiger Moth, Leopard Moth, Hornet Moth, Dragonfly, Fox Moth and Dragon Rapide. The last two were painted in the livery used by the King's Flight in the 1930s, with the Prince of Wales feathers on their rudders. How privileged I was!

It was not long before Barry realised that it was not just flying lessons that attracted me to Martin. He was very reasonable about it, but rather sad, when he challenged me on the subject, and I had to admit that Martin was no longer just my pilot. He said I had to choose between the two of them; I chose – but we parted company as friends. As a goodbye gift I gave him several pieces of carthorse saddlery and haynes that I had rescued from the stable at Melbury and kept as souvenirs. He was delighted.

Brian Woodford was a very rich man. His main business was based in Singapore, where he and his second wife, a Chinese lady called Laura, lived in a luxury 'condominium'. He also operated from a mansion in Fort Worth, Texas, and was in the process of having a large holiday house built in Colorado. He had made his fortune dealing mainly in aircraft spares, chiefly for helicopters. He was a very generous and gregarious host and had many Texan friends. Every August a gang of these would descend upon Chalmington Manor to have fun. The main event each year was to attend the de Havilland Moth Club's annual fly-in held at the Duke of Bedford's grass airstrip at Woburn Abbey. His whole fleet of de Havillands would attend – and for several years he won the cup for the most beautifully restored aeroplane there. It always seemed to be a sunny day, and in the evening there followed a banquet in the Statue Gallery, with a jazz band. All this was paid for by Brian, as were the costs of our hotel rooms in Woburn village. Everything was meticulously organised by Brian's 'ADC', Arthur Cole, who lived in a part of Chalmington Manor with his wife Edna and ran the office there, being in contact with Brian daily by fax wherever he happened to be working. Arthur also organised visits to air shows, earning some income from providing displays. I attended all those at which Martin was flying, and Brian always paid all our hotel expenses. One of our most popular attendances was the annual air show at Badminton House, where the Duchess of Beaufort generously provided hospitality for visiting pilots and aircraft owners.

Once my first flying season petered out in late autumn, I continued to see Martin pretty regularly and I found we had lots more in common – not just aeroplanes but also steam railways, old motor cars and motor racing, canals and many other eccentric things. By now he knew several of my friends and family and we both dined with my cousins, the Pisanis, on Christmas night. Martin had arranged to visit friends in Yorkshire for New Year. He was due to be away for four or five days, and after he had left to go north I suddenly realised that I missed him badly. I had expected him to return on the 3rd or 4th of January – but he suddenly came back to me on the 2nd, so I hoped that might be because he missed me too!

Martin Holloway was one of the third or fourth generation of a family building firm, Holloway Brothers. Three brothers had set up as builders early in the late nineteenth century in Wiltshire, but were so successful that they decided to move to London. There they continued to prosper and were responsible for some of the most prestigious buildings in the city, including The Old Bailey, the Bank of England, Whiteleys department store in Bayswater, The Ritz hotel, Chelsea Bridge and Caversham Bridge among others.

They also had contracts abroad, one of which was the construction of the first bridge across the Tigris at Baghdad.

Martin's father, Laurence Holloway, was at one time President of the Institute of Building and he was also a senior freemason. It was intended that both Martin and his twin brother, Colin, would follow him into the business after their education at Oundle and the London College of Building. However, Holloway Brothers was taken over by Laing in the 1960s, and for a time Martin worked for the builders, Wates, on housing projects. But he really had other ideas. He was determined on a flying career. At school he'd joined the Air Cadets and he was awarded a flying scholarship by the RAF. He had learnt to fly in a Tiger Moth at Skegness, on a strip beside Butlin's Holiday Camp, where he stayed whilst training. He then went on to join the Fleet Air Arm, where he graduated to flying Buccaneer bombers off HMS *Eagle*. He was one of those who bombed the beached Torrey Canyon oil tanker in the attempt to set her on fire and prevent pollution of the nearby beaches. Later he was to fly Hunters as targets for the Royal Navy, operating from Lossiemouth in Scotland for North Atlantic exercises, from Yeovilton over the Channel and from Gibraltar around the Mediterranean. At that time he was one of the Hunter pilots in the Fleet Air Arm's aerobatic display team, the Blue Herons. After leaving the navy, he was for a few years a 'bus driver' with a couple of commercial airlines, flying the ill-fated Comet.

Life was then very kind to Martin and he was recruited by Airwork on behalf of the Royal Navy to fly their communications aircraft, the Jetstream, used for ferrying senior officers, politicians, VIPs and naval personnel to destinations as far afield as Bardufoss in the north of Norway and to Gibraltar for operations in the Mediterranean and to the Canary Islands. One of the Jetstream's other uses, for those based at Culdrose in Cornwall, was for the training of navigators. These aircraft were fitted with special navigational equipment. Obviously navigators need to be trained to fly through foreign airspace, so trips were made to several European destinations, to which the Yeovilton team would accompany the training team and their students. Wives and girlfriends were allowed to go along on some of these trips too. For me, loving to fly even in large airliners, to fly in one as small as the Jetstream with only eighteen passengers over the Alps and the Pyrennees was a thrill in itself, but in addition we visited and stayed a couple of days in each of several interesting cities, including Barcelona, Prague, Valetta, Lisbon and Stavanger. This last era of Martin's career sadly came to an end when he reached retirement age. Now he only had his own aeroplane to fly.

Back at Chalmington, with Brian and Laura based in Fort Worth, Arthur and Edna were invited to pay a visit to the Texan mansion. A party had been arranged to welcome them and it was in full swing when Arthur suddenly began to feel unwell. Within a couple of hours he keeled over and died. Obviously this was a shattering blow to Brian, who had known Arthur since way back in the war. Not only had he lost a friend, but he'd also lost someone on whom he relied totally to look after his domestic affairs and manage his aircraft, motorcar and motorcycle collections. It was more than a tragedy; it was a catastrophe.

Brian and Laura returned to England that August, with a party of friends, and fortunately Edna was there to run the household for them. I had just been given the sack from the PR firm and Martin asked me if I thought I could and would like to take on Arthur's job. It would be the chance of a lifetime, I thought. So Martin took Brian on one side and suggested that I might be a suitable replacement. Brian agreed and briefed me about his quite complex ways of working. By then I owned a rather basic Amstrad computer, which I offered to use in the office – previously there had only been an ancient manual typewriter there. The office consisted of two rooms on the second floor of the manor, with a large desk facing the window and overlooking the swimming pool, garden and airstrip. It was fantastic and I was very excited when I installed myself and re-arranged the office. The second room housed the fax machine and photocopier. Once Brian had returned to Singapore in September, I was in daily contact with him by fax.

When I climbed up to my attic each morning, my first task was to check all Brian's faxes and carry out any instructions he had given me. Most of these were trivial domestic items, but he always liked me to confirm that I had carried them out immediately. I was proud to have Wessex & Aviation Transport cards with 'Mrs Jane Donaldson, Director' printed on them.

Other members of the domestic staff who did not live in were a housemaid, her husband the gardener, and a handyman. Working with the collections were an engineer and a voluntary ex-Westland engineer, Keith Pardoe. Then, of course, there were the pilots. The atmosphere in the hangar's crew room was always cheerful and some of the pilots would turn up not necessarily to fly but to help with maintenance and cleaning of the fleet. I usually spent my lunch hour drinking coffee and chatting in the crew room with anyone who happened to be working there.

I settled in very well and loved my work, but there was one big problem. Edna Cole. Understandably, Edna was still deeply mourning the loss of her husband, and perhaps part of this meant that she resented the fact that someone else, and a woman at that, had taken over Arthur's job – which I think she felt in some way demeaned her own position in the whole Chalmington set-up. She made it her job to undermine me whenever she could, which was not very pleasant but I did my best to be charming to her all the same. It was the only way to defeat her and I was able to ignore her inter-ference for quite a long time and just get on with my job.

Brian had briefed me that he really needed to increase the 'earn-ings' of the fleet by getting more bookings for air shows, films and advertising shoots etc. He realised that this meant it was imperative that all the aircraft were kept airworthy and gleaming clean, so he decided to employ a full-time, experienced engineer qualified to carry out annual inspections and to sign the necessary paperwork. The engineer moved into a bungalow on the estate with his wife. He'd had his own small engineering works in the North, but had closed it down by then. He was a bluff character, but he was rather a 'hit it with a hammer' engineer. He was also impossible at paperwork, and this did cause tension between us. I would inform him each time I achieved an air show booking, only to discover when checking with him closer to the actual date of the event that the aircraft's CofA (Certificate of Airworthiness) had expired or the aircraft itself was unserviceable. This left me with the task of apologising and pacifying the air show managers involved.

While I was working for Brian, he was hungry for more veteran motorcars and was attending many auctions. There was always celebration when a new car arrived on a transporter. One day a steam-driven car arrived. Brian had already recruited another Brian – Brian Casely – to look after the cars, although I remained responsible for making sure they were all MOTd and re-taxed punctually. This Brian had a steam car of his own, so he was quite excited at the prospect of this new arrival for the motorhouse, and he quickly earned the nickname of 'Steamer'. We all loved Steamer, and he was one of the nicest characters I worked alongside at Chalmington.

In spite of many, many irritations I did manage to earn considerably more fees for appearances and displays at air shows. The Rapide featured in a *Poirot* TV programme and the Fox Moth in an episode of the TV series *House of Eliott*.

There was great excitement one year when a young visiting Texan couple wanted to be married in England and in particular to be married in Cattistock Church, with their reception to be held at Chalmington Manor. This needed permission from the Archbishop of Canterbury as neither the groom nor the bride-to-be were resident in this country, and furthermore they were foreigners. I had to negotiate with the Archbishop's office, which finally agreed to make an exception for the couple. American weddings are not at all the same as ours. No hats for the women and no morning coats for the men. There were frantic expeditions to Dorchester for the ladies to find hats and the men to be fitted out with morning coats and top hats. No one had thought to brief the father of the bride that it was usual for top hats to be removed at the entrance to the church; his remained on his head as he accompanied his daughter down the aisle and it stayed there throughout the service!

On another occasion meriting a celebration, the Woodfords decided to throw a large party. The house was perfect for such an event, with its large entrance hall (its walls papered with one of the Pugin-designed wallpapers used in the Houses of Parliament) and a very big drawing room for pre-dinner drinking. Early on, Laura consulted me about the arrangements and asked me to organise caterers, table and chair hire etc. I had often been asked by her to do the flowers in the reception and dining areas of the house and I used to lend her one or two of my own large vases because she had none of her own. Obviously my brief was to do the flowers for this party – only on a much larger scale than usual. Brian told me he would deal with the ordering of the wines, but he asked me to prepare the seating plan. The guests would be a mixture of Texans, his flying and motoring friends, pilots and a couple of neighbours. I already knew of excellent caterers, Pipfield, whom I'd met several times at other people's parties, and I invited them to provide a menu and a quotation. Everything was going nicely according to plan so far. The day for final preparations arrived and I bought lots of lovely summer flowers and provided some from my own garden to add to those the Chalmington gardener had given me. Eventually all the rooms were ready and the flower arrangements looked beautiful. The caterers had arrived and were beavering away in the kitchen. I went up to my office to change and leave plenty of time for any last-minute hitches.

When I went downstairs, all glammed up, I was met by a screaming, ranting, raging Laura clutching my table plan and crossing things out telling me it was all wrong. There were two circular tables in the hall as well as those in the dining room. I had previously discussed my plan with Brian, who had approved it without amendment. The mistake I had made, in Laura's eyes, was to mix the Woodfords' personal guests with 'the workers' – i.e. Martin and myself, the Chief Engineer and his wife and a few pilots and their partners and other 'outsiders'. On Laura's revised list, all of us, the peasants, were seated together in the hall. As it happened, we were the winners as we had much more fun being all together.

However, everything went off splendidly, and at about 10 p.m. The Yetties arrived and kept us entertained until the small hours. Brian did apologise to me about the seating cock-up – Laura always got her own way.

The next development was the arrival of 'wing walker' Caroline. Caroline already had a job as receptionist at a PR agency in Bristol, but she had a feeling that she was going to be made redundant. When Brian heard this he suggested she might come and work with me in the Chalmington office. She was allowed to purchase a brand new and more up-to-date computer, a smart typist's desk and more filing cabinets. We re-arranged the office and Caroline moved in. Adjoining the office was a large double bedroom, and Caroline moved in there too.

Brian's attitude to me had recently begun to change and there were several incidents and misunderstandings about parking and other trivial matters. I honestly think this happened because he realised, quite rightly, that there was not enough work for two in the office. I also think that he hoped that I would not get on with Caroline – but in fact we got on wonderfully well. She was a charming creature and we enjoyed each other's company and worked as a good team. However, I suspected that Brian would really like to get rid of me, so I thought I'd better put feelers out to find a job elsewhere.

Chapter Twenty

Quite by chance – it must have been ESP – I wrote to Richard Timmis and told him I was looking for another job and asked if any of his contacts in the business world of Yeovil might be looking for a secretary. He replied – not quite with whoops of joy, but certainly with enthusiasm – and told me that his present secretary was just about to leave. I went and had a chat with him in his office and we were both enthusiastic at the prospect of my return. There was one problem though: Richard had handed over the office administration to his son, Nigel, and Nigel would not agree to match the salary I was getting at Wessex Aviation, although Richard himself would have been happy to do so. I suggested that he might meet me halfway by allowing me the same privileges as those I'd enjoyed previously. These were: (a) free use of his Menorca villa for two weeks a year out of season and Gonzales, his 2CV Citroen we'd used on our last visits there, and (b) the occasional loan of his large house at East Portlemouth, across the water from Salcombe in Devon. He also agreed that I need not start work in the mornings until 10 a.m. This was indeed a lucky move for me.

I had actually reached retirement age by then and was working on a self-employed basis. This left me free also to work for other people in a freelance capacity. I called myself 'Copycat Management Services', had business cards printed and placed a couple of advertisements in *The Literary Review*. This brought forth fruit from the

E.F. Benson Society and a very interesting project transferring old editions of their newsletters onto floppy discs. I also worked for my clever step-daughter, Alison, a management consultant. She had a very large project in progress, interviewing chief executives of major companies and taping their conversations. I would then transcribe these interviews onto floppy discs and she would produce articles for publication. There was also work to be had from architects, because I was conversant with construction-speak. I wrote copy for a stately home's brochure and for a plant hire company – two very different assignments!

Then, by pure coincidence, the best-ever introduction came my way. Since I was a schoolgirl I had been a fan of the writings of Evelyn Waugh, and in my twenties I went on to enjoy those of his son Auberon. I'd bought a copy of *The Foxglove Saga* when it first came out in 1960 and loved it. I knew that he lived at Combe Florey near Taunton, and when I'd settled down in Somerset I decide to write to him asking if I might call upon him with my copy of his book and if he would autograph it for me. He replied suggesting I should telephone and he'd be pleased to see me. A date was arranged and we drove to Combe Florey in Martin's Lagonda bearing a bottle of Champagne and *The Foxglove Saga*. We were most courteously received by Auberon in his study, the bottle was opened and we talked with him for a good half hour. He kindly wrote in my book: 'For Jane Donaldson, Souvenir of a visit to Combe Florey and in particular for the Champagne. Auberon Waugh, Combe Florey House, Taunton, March 12 1989'. Before we left, he showed us all round the ground floor of the house and said he was sorry his wife Teresa had not been there to meet us and that he hoped we could visit again when she was at home.

Not a long time afterwards, my sister Carol attended a reunion at her old school, St Michael's, Limpsfield. Chatting to an old school friend, Amanda, Caroline learnt with interest that she worked for Auberon Waugh and that she and her husband lived in part of the house at Combe Florey. Amanda said she loved her job, but she found it almost impossible to get away for weekends or holidays because Bron said he couldn't do without her. Carol then had a brainwave. She told Amanda that she was sure I would be more than happy to stand in for her. The plan was put to Auberon, and he agreed. We had a great system whereby he would fax me his handwritten copy for 'Way of The World', his regular column in *The Daily Telegraph*, I would decipher it and type it up, then fax the typescript back to him for any amendments – which usually meant cutting it down; he was only allowed 1,000 words. Another fax would come back to me with his alterations and I would produce the final version and e-mail it to Sarah Sands at *The Telegraph*. Every now and then we'd have hiccups, because Bron was not too handy with a fax machine and very occasionally his neighbour would have to help out!

Bron did invite us back to Combe Florey again, for Sunday lunchtime drinks with his family and his beloved Pekineses to whom he kept feeding nibbles, much against family orders. One hot summer Sunday I gave a luncheon party in my garden with just a few of our closest friends. Bron and Teresa were able to come too – I felt very honoured that they joined us. During a conversation with Martin, Teresa said she would love to have a flight in the Stampe, and later that summer Martin took her up. She was thrilled to fly over Combe Florey and to see her house from the air. Bron thought she was quite mad! Sadly his health was beginning to fail by then, and a photograph that was taken of him standing beside me in my garden at that party, wearing one of my sun-hats, shows he had lost much weight and was looking a little gaunt. After he died in January 2000 we went to his funeral in Bishop's Lydiard. It was a huge funeral and police were there in force to help control the traffic. Bron loved to write tauntingly about the police, and this must often have irritated them. However, as his cortège was driven to the church, every policeman lining the route stood to attention and saluted as he passed by. It was a very moving sight.

When my mother died in 2000, at the age of ninety, I was lucky enough to benefit from trusts set up by both my Auld and Keelan grandparents. I therefore no longer needed to work quite so hard and only took on projects that particularly interested me. The chief, and last, of these was the transcribing of the handwritten diaries of a country gentleman who lived in the eighteenth and nineteenth centuries. Not only were these diaries a record of his shooting and fishing achievements, but also, as a separate volume, a record of his military service under the Duke of Wellington in the Peninsular War. My client's biography of this man has yet to be completed by him, but regretfully I had to say that I no longer felt like working – at seventy-five I wanted to enjoy a life of leisure. I had been working solidly since 1950. Enough was enough.

Chapter Twenty-one

As I write today, it is twenty-six years since I first met Martin. A way of life has evolved that suits us both perfectly. We each keep our own attractive thatched cottages, with only about six miles between them. Neither cottage is large enough for the two of us to share, as we both have a lot of furniture, pictures, books and lots of the junk that most people collect over the years. We spend evenings and weekends together, but during the week I can see my girlfriends, play bridge, do gardening, shopping, reading etc. Martin can do what he likes to do – working on his garden, his aeroplane or his cars. Not only does he have his 1931 Lagonda, which he's owned for over forty years, but he also has a 'Saintmobile' – a Volvo P1800 sports car – as well as his late-father's large Rover and a tiny Fiat Uno daily runabout. Fortunately he has a large, thatched garage and plenty of parking space as well.

Over the years we have on several occasions flown the Stampe to Belgium and to France – we've even been as far south as Brive in the Dordogne in her. Crossing the Channel in a single-engined sixty-year old aeroplane is a fairly daunting experience, but we've always been lucky and we take the shortest possible route – from Sandown in the Isle of Wight to Cap Griz Nez or from Compton Abbas in Dorset to Cherbourg. We both enjoy the same eccentric things – steam railways, canals, old cars and motorbikes, old houses and our many friends. We belong to the West Somerset Railway, The Lynton & Barnstaple Railway and The Croydon Airport Society – and, of course, the Lagonda Club and the Vintage Sports Car Club. Attending various events relating to these clubs gives us plenty of enjoyable company and meeting up with old friends with similar enthusiasms. We usually go to France once or twice a year, to visit my step-granddaughter Georgina, her French husband Marc and their six-year-old son, Balthazaar. They live in an old farmhouse near Fontevraud, between Saumur and Chinon. Other friends with whom we stay live quite near Le Mans, so not too far away.

I think one of the best things, for me, of being at home and not working is that I can spend more time with my animals. I am besotted with both cats and dogs. Stupid people say that one is either a cat person or a dog person. I don't think that is true. I love both, equally. When I came to Hinton St George I no longer had a dog, but I still had four cats: Tesco, Sainsbury, Waitrose and Tabasco. As this first gang died, one by one, I added two more black and whites – Lea and Perrins. Lea, a female, soon became 'Flea' (named after a small French aeroplane called The Flying Flea) and she produced two litters of kittens. My theme for the new generation was aircraft – so I now had Spitfire, Hurricane and Mosquito. Inevitably, over the thirty-three years I have lived in Somerset, even these newer additions grew old. The last of them to survive was Mosquito, who became Fluffy-Boy because he was very fluffy. He was the naughtiest cat I have ever owned. He was not a tom (I'd had him neutered), but he sprayed *everywhere*. My house stank of cats' pee – no, that's an exaggeration, but he did mark a lot of furniture with his spraying, and after he was dead I had to spend a lot of money on restoration. His worst effort took place when my drawing room was being redecorated and all the dog pictures were temporarily stacked in my office, against walls and covered with dust sheets. My finest picture is one of coursing greyhounds. It is large and usually hangs above the fireplace. Fluffy managed to get behind the dust sheet and deposit a squirt of spray over the lower part of the picture and frame. Because 'damage caused by domestic pets' is not covered by insurance, this mischief cost me over £1,000 to repair.

All the cats and dogs who have died here are buried in my garden and have headstones. It's like an animal cemetery, but I enjoy feeling that they are all still close to me. I now only have one cat. Black and white, again, and a rescue queen from Ferne Animal Sanctuary, near Chard. She was called Fifi when I got her, and Fifi she remains.

Once I was really settled in at my cottage I began yearning for a dog. Fate did a good job and found one for me. My Aunt Pamela had been to a drinks party at a farmhouse in Devon one evening at which there was a black whippet sitting on a sofa. The farmer had recently been widowed and planned to leave the farm and move to a small bungalow in another village. The whippet had really been his late-wife's dog and had been used to roaming loose around the farm. The farmer was concerned that the dog might get run over once he had moved to a situation near a road, and he felt it best to find a home for it. Pam immediately thought of me, and told the farmer she would find out whether I would give the dog a home. Of course, I said I would. With only a day or two's delay, we set off in my car to collect him. He settled down on the back seat and we chatted our way back to my cottage. Pam had forgotten about a bar of Kit-Kat that was in her jacket pocket, and when she got out of the car she found the wrapper in shreds on the floor beneath the whippet. He had surreptitiously dragged if from Pam's pocket and devoured it. Whippets are dreadful thieves.

I had named him 'Rampy', short for Rampisham, after the village in which I had rented Keeper's Cottage. I was again lucky with my jobs and was always able to take Rampy to work with me. Richard Timmis's office was furnished with a black leather sofa and armchairs and he allowed Rampy to sleep on them. Occasionally either Richard or a visitor would not notice a black dog on a black sofa and Rampy would nearly get sat on. He lived to quite an old age and he got thinner and thinner and began having a series of small strokes, from which he would quickly recover. But these strokes became more and more frequent and the vet and I agreed, after he took a long time to recover from one, that he should be put to sleep.

After a short period of mourning I was lucky to find another whippet, a rescue dog from a broken family who could no longer keep him. I called this one Monty, after nearby Montacute House. He was a dark brindle colour and extremely handsome – and his only bad habit was theft. He could even jump onto the kitchen table and eat the cats' food. He loved outings in the Lagonda. He would sit on my lap in the front, securely tied to me in case he might jump out after a rabbit or a squirrel. Monty was an even more voracious thief than Rampy. We were never able to train him.

After Monty died I had great difficulty finding a replacement from a rescue centre. I was told that they seldom got whippets – but plenty of ex-racing greyhounds – because whippets are very rarely badly treated or given away. After a year of struggling I decided I would have to get my next dog from a breeder. And so it was that we found ourselves travelling to Port Talbot in Wales to meet our next and naughtiest companion. He was only six months old and a very destructive puppy. He devoured shoes, two television wands, a walkie-talkie telephone, a couple of books and, worst of all, one of my hugely expensive hearing aids, although now he is four and he has calmed down a lot. We named him 'George III', because he is completely mad and also my third whippet. We look forward to many more years of pleasure with him. He and Fifi get on well, although Fifi has complete control over him and keeps him at bay.

I cannot complete these memoirs without revealing how being with Martin has given me the wonderful new presence of his grown-up daughters and their families, who increasingly give me enormous pleasure. By his former wife Martin had three girls: Claire, Alexandra and Georgia. They were in their twenties when I first met them, and I really got to know them properly once they had each married exceptionally interesting and loveable husbands and settled down. I am now blessed with a very rewarding extended family, with four young grandsons and the prettiest of grand-daughters. Martin has given me so much...

I started to write these memoirs in 1979 – so they have had a long gestation period. The task has enabled me to re-live my life, thanks to my extraordinary detailed memory for events – but unfortunately my memory for names increasingly lets me down! By the time this book is published I shall be eighty – but thanks to my good health I feel just as young, rebellious and mischievous as I did in my twenties.

I have never wanted children, and in my twenties and thirties found them rather a nuisance. I could not stand babies; always crying or being sick. Now that I am old I find babies quite adorable and children rather fun to be with. Of course, in my day children were seen-and-not-heard, so we found it difficult to relate to grown-ups – indeed, grown-ups were our enemies. Nowadays children are treated quite differently, and mostly that's a great step forward. I have several adult step-children, and their children, in my own and my 'step-families', and they do encourage me to believe that although the world will continue to change, for good and bad, they will all cope well with whatever lies ahead – they'll have to!

I was a Saturday's child and, yes, I have worked hard for my living – but I have been lucky to enjoy all the many jobs of my working life. I like retirement even more, and I look back and think how fortunate I was to have been born in the 1930s. I would hate to be young in the twenty-first century. So much that was good has vanished, and so many of the new things that have arrived are, to me, horrible. I hate denim. Why does everybody want to look like a down-at heel peasant? Why do people put hideous 'trainers' on their feet? What on earth has happened to popular music? How come droning, wailing and boom-boom-boom have replaced the smooth dance-bands, crooners and trad jazz bands of my youth? I simply cannot understand it. Nor can I understand why people have to be in constant contact with each other – with mobile phones clamped to their ears and musical stethoscopes plugged into them, even when shopping in supermarkets. And as for Facebook and doing everything 'on-line', it is unfriendly, foreign territory to me.

I am sickened by the proliferation of split infinitives, even in quality newspapers and magazines. Many well-educated journalists, whom I presume have degrees in English, are guilty of this ugly treatment of our language. I dare say I have been guilty in my memoir of some grammatical faults myself – if so, I apologise to those who have been offended by my ignorance!

Language leads me on to pronunciation. Why is it now 'garridge' instead of garage? 'Reesearch' instead of research? OK; so I'm pedantic – and proud of it! I could go on and on . . .

Of course, many are the good things, too, and I suppose it must be good that a much broader section of the population is able to take advantage of these, whereas in the days of my youth it was only 'people like us' who enjoyed most of the better things in life. We hear so much about the 'youth of today' being philistine, thoughtless and bad mannered – but I am glad to say that all those young people with whom my paths cross give great pleasure to me, and I feel that the country I eventually leave behind me is going to be left in good hands.

Inevitably, I have not managed to write about all my friends and family; that would be impossible in just one book about myself. However, once *Plain Jane* has been finally polished up and put to bed, I suspect that I may be tempted back to my inspirational word-processor. There are still, I hope, quite a few more years ahead for new adventures . . .